The Ben Book

Michael Galvin

The Ben Book
A father's memoir

The Ben Book: A father's memoir
ISBN 978 1 76041 886 1
Copyright © Michael Galvin 2020

First published 2020 by
GINNINDERRA PRESS
PO Box 3461 Port Adelaide 5015
www.ginninderrapress.com.au

Contents

Introduction		7
1	The Angel of History	11
2	Paradise Lost	22
3	Beach Scenes From the 1950s	37
4	100 Millilitres of Water, 24 Grams of Life	52
5	It Can't Be Helped	63
6	Panic Attack	77
7	From Son to Mate, and Back Again	88
8	Losing Ben	102
9	Aristotle Makes a Statement	116
10	Rip Van Winkle	133
References		160

Introduction

Benjamin died on 26 June 2007, more than ten years ago, at the time of writing this.

Perhaps that seems a long time to take to tell his tale. But anyone reading this will know that neither trauma nor grief has a mechanical, let alone a predictable, chronology. Minutes, days or years – they all lose their customary meaning.

While much of the memoir that follows was written in the first years after Ben's death, it has taken me this time to be able to face up to its publication.

By the end of the first chapter, the reader will already know the main events and milestones in Ben's twenty-two years of life, a life lived with the disease known as Duchenne muscular dystrophy. What I have tried to do thereafter is to provide insight into what it means to live with a serious physical disability, what my son meant to me, and what it means to have lost him. Most of all, I want to bear witness to the realities of my son's life, and to put into words the respect and love I have for him. I hope that my experiences might be of value and maybe even some comfort to anyone who finds themselves in a similar position.

The incidents described in this discontinuous narrative are to the best of my knowledge and memory.

On one level, Benjamin Bede Galvin lived his own unique and special life. As his father, I coped (or did not cope) as best I could with being his father, and my story is also an idiosyncratic one. Yet on another level, we are both representative of concentration points of our times. Benjamin was a textbook case of a boy, and then a young man, with Duchenne muscular dystrophy, and what it means to live and die from this disease, in Australia, in suburban Adelaide, at the end of the twentieth century and the beginning of the twenty-first. And I am his ageing baby boomer father, handed a script I cannot change very much, from the moment of diagnosis when he was a year old, to the present moment, when I cannot imagine any future day in my life when I will not feel some pain of his loss.

I have done my best to write for at least two types of reader: a reader involved in the muscular dystrophy community on the one hand; and a reader who has not been personally involved in the world of disability on the other. This presents any writer in this situation with some challenging questions, to do with privacy, good taste, sentimentality, mawkishness, the stories of others involved, the balance between sharing information and over-sharing too much information, to name some of them. If I have gone too far, I hope the reader will forgive my lapses in judgement.

Finally, Benjamin was known and loved by many people, but by no one more than by his mother Esther and his sister Rosanna. While I know my words can never make up for what is now as lost in their lives as it is in mine, I dedicate this book to their happy memories of wonderful times with a remarkable son and brother, whose good humour and acceptance in the face of adversity will never be forgotten.

A brief note on names and naming

When Benjamin was born, he was given the name Benjamin Bede. Bede came from my grandfather, Donald Bede Galvin, whose memory I wished to honour. Benjamin came from nowhere in particular. But of course we were part of a trend without knowing it, and it later seemed as if every second boy born in Sydney in the mid-1980s was called Benjamin too. We knew that this name would often be shortened to Ben, so there were many times when I heard his mother say to people, 'It's Benji, not Ben.' So Benjamin was a Benji in the early years of his life, and many of those who mainly knew him when he was young still refer to him as Benji. However, by the time he was in high school, more and more people, including most of my family, were calling him Ben. From about eighteen onwards, he was a Ben to me and his sister, and most of his friends. In this book, when I am imagining the times when he was a Benjamin or Benji to me, I will call him that. And when there are times when he was a Ben to me, I will call him that too.

1

The Angel of History

Late November 2004

Ben and I are in a blue Volkswagen van, heading east along the Murray Valley Highway in Victoria. It is a hot, sunny November day in this part of the country.

If you had been in an aeroplane flying overhead, we would have been one of the black dots you could see down below. At that height and speed, the past, present and future tend to blur. You can see black dots like us, cars, trucks and vans, approaching each other before we do. It is a strange feeling. You can fly through a weather front and know what tomorrow is going to be like where you have just left.

We are on our way from Adelaide to Albury-Wodonga to take part in a weekend of electric wheelchair sports with others from SA, NSW, Victoria and the ACT. About thirty teenagers and young men will be there. All have some form of muscular dystrophy. All face the same prognosis: an ongoing wasting away of their muscles, beginning at conception and leading to an early death.

It was hot in Nigel's van that day. We were travelling together because his van is big enough to take his son, Callum (then thirteen), as well as Ben (just turned twenty) and me, and all the associated gear and baggage. Ben's chair was furthest from the air conditioning. Whether he was uncomfortable in that long drive in the heat, in the back of the van, with nothing really to look at, we will never know. Ben did not complain about such things. Not then, not ever. If I had expressed concern in front of his young teammate, he would have mumbled something to the effect, 'Leave me alone, Dad. I'll deal with it.'

It's a long journey – a thousand kilometres in a day. After several hours of undulating mallee country between South Australia and Vic- toria, the highway reaches the Murray River near a shady town called Tooleybuc. A left turn takes you across the river, north to Balranald, over the empty Hay Plain, and on to Sydney; a right turn ushers in a very different experience – a journey along the Murray Valley Highway, through settled, irrigated Victoria, through charming river towns like Swan Hill and Echuca.

What were you feeling that day, Ben, when we got to the familiar turn-off on the highway? Were your feelings like mine? Sadness and regret that so many family trips to Sydney through Tooleybuc were now a thing of the past? Or also a sense of excitement about seeing something new and different? Your parents' marriage had ended a few months before. What that really meant for all of us, for everything, was only slowly sinking in. Speeding along the Murray Valley Highway that afternoon, you and I were both carrying as much baggage in our heads and hearts as in the van itself.

The occasional plane flies overhead. In my mind's eye, I can visualise what little black moving dots like us down below must look like, hardly appearing to move when seen from that height. I can see two such dots, one of them us, moving eastwards on the highway. I can see another one, moving southwards, on one of the many roads that cross this highway at right angles. I can see the future about to happen.

The crash of metal tearing into metal echoes through the trees and disturbs the flocks of shrieking galahs.

A middle-aged woman is lying close to death in the hot and smoking wreck of her car. We slow down as we pass by, saying little, thinking much, a blue tarpaulin about to obscure her from view. A few minutes earlier, and that would have been us. Death has swooped down today into this benign pastoral paradise. Death has seemingly come from nowhere on this highway, and chosen this woman, yet it came so close to choosing all of us.

I don't believe in angels, but I do need some representational form for death, the way it can come so close, hover in the air, feel as real as any person present, but not take you then and there, and you live on. We felt the flutter of the angel of death's wings that afternoon on the highway. But we had been spared.

A few months pass. I am with Ben after an appointment with a specialist at the Queen Elizabeth Hospital in Adelaide. We are going towards the entrance on our way out, when I notice a work colleague standing alongside and bending over a patient in a hospital chair. He is ministering to this woman, his wife. I had only met her once before – a strong, confident, beautiful woman in the prime of her life. Time seems to suddenly stop, as Ben and I move past. Words are impossible. She is now so ravaged by the dying process that my heart seems to miss a beat the moment I realise this spectral wraith, this skeleton, is her. We are back on that highway again from the previous summer.

Death returns to check Ben out again twice in the next two years, comes right up close, breathes on him, takes his breath away, puts him in hospital for two long stints, but then notices someone else and moves on. But inevitably, on 26 June 2007, the angel returns again, and this time there is no mistake, no second chance. It's my son's time.

The German writer Theodor Adorno once reflected on what it means to run on a city street. Such running is so unusual that it suggests some kind of internal or external crisis – the existential fear and panic accompanying a terrorist attack, for example. Adorno was right. Normal people in normal clothes don't run in the street unless there is something abnormal going on. I've only run like this twice – wildly, desperately, panic setting in.

The first time was in the early years after Benji had finally started walking. While he did manage to walk for a few years, he didn't have the strength to actually run or jump. More worryingly, his ability to stay on his feet was fragile and unstable. If he fell over, he fell like a tree, often landing flat on his face, knocking himself out, and his breathing would stop. These falls happened every few months for a couple of years when he was an infant. The first time it happened, I thought he was dead or dying, and ran with his limp, unconscious body in my arms to the neighbour's front door. By the time I got there, he had come to and his breathing had started again. Doctors assured us that this was relatively 'normal', and not to worry too much about it.

The second time I ran in terror was around 10.30 p.m. on Tuesday night, 26 June 2007. Half an hour earlier, I had been in bed reading an Elizabeth George crime novel when I got a call from one of the staff at the Julia Farr Centre. The caller said that Ben, who had only just arrived back from spending the day with me at my house, had had some kind of collapse, and was at that moment being transported in an ambulance to the emergency department at Royal Adelaide Hospital. After the call, I phoned his mother with this news, got myself dressed, and drove to the hospital. I was concerned, but not overly so. Ben had been in hospital often enough to blunt the effect of being told that he was on his way there again.

It was only as I was parking the car on a side street, several hundred metres from the emergency ward, that it suddenly hit me. The woman on the phone from Julia Farr had used the word 'intubated'. It had taken thirty minutes for that dreaded word to register in my consciousness. Once it did, I ran from the car along North Terrace to the emergency ward, shaking with fear.

The entrance and waiting area to the emergency ward felt like most such places would feel on a cold, damp night in the middle of a metropolis. People in the waiting room were hanging around in various states of distress or boredom. The woman on duty was still trying to take down my particulars when a doctor came rushing towards me, asked me who I was, and took me with him back into the inner rooms of the ward, the paperwork still sitting uncompleted on the front desk.

Benjamin was in a bed. His eyes were closed and he looked asleep. He was hooked up to machines that keep your lungs breathing and your heart beating, and he was intubated just as I had been told, the tube into his lungs going in via his mouth. In those first few moments,

I had no clear idea how serious the situation was. There were a lot of people around, and the only word from the doctor in charge that I can remember from that first period while standing next to Ben, and holding him, was 'unstable' – as in, every vital sign right now is 'unstable'. Is that word casualty room code for 'near death' (or even dead)? I did not take that in if it was.

(I also did not notice whether the monitor showing his vital signs was turned on or off. Joan Didion notes in one of her books that emergency room practice in the United States is to turn away or even turn off the screens at such times; family members sometimes tend to watch the screen for signs of life, rather than focus on the last minutes of the dying person they are with.)

There was a small room not far away, and the doctor took me there as soon as he could, sat me down and started to talk quickly and in earnest. He told me that the situation was very serious, that it was touch and go whether Ben would pull through, that something massive seemed to have happened, like a cerebral haemorrhage, that the ambulance crew had worked for more than thirty minutes to get his heart started again, that Ben's brain, if he lived, would have been permanently damaged from being this long without oxygen. He also reminded me that Ben was a twenty-two-year-old male with Duchenne muscular dystrophy, and that he was therefore a low priority for an intensive care bed in any hospital in Adelaide that night. The main thing I realised he was telling me was to get ready to decide whether – or, more realistically, when – the life support equipment should be turned off. I said that I didn't want to make any decisions until his mother had arrived and she and I could talk about it.

I went back to Ben, this time shaking with the knowledge that his life was almost certainly ebbing out of him, even though he looked peaceful and asleep, just as I had seen him thousands of times before. Esther arrived. We stood on each side of our son, and held him tightly. We each held one of his hands, our other hands joined across his chest. I was dimly aware that my tears were dropping onto the white sheet over his chest. The doctor reminded us of the decision we had to make, and we went back into the nondescript meeting room I had been in a few minutes before.

We had hardly had enough time to sit down when this same doctor came rushing back in. This time he was running.

'I think you should come back now. We're losing him.'

Esther and I resumed our positions alongside Ben. I was on his left, she was on his right. We both held him by each hand. We told him how much we loved him. We both felt a faint squeeze from him in the hands we were holding. Ben had heard us, we were sure of that. Ben knew we were there. Trauma does terrible things to your memory, so the fact that we both remembered this faint squeeze of our hand makes me think it really did happen.

If there can be such a thing, Benjamin Bede Galvin, my son and my friend, died a beautiful death. From the moment he was born, he was encompassed in unconditional love from both his parents, a love he was aware of and was sustained by. He passed away feeling this same love, feeling no pain or distress. I cannot say if there was a precise moment when he stopped breathing. If there was, it was understated, not dramatic in any way. It is a cliché, but it was as if he was just continuing to slumber, at peace with himself and the world.

The nurses who were there that night were more presences than people, moving quietly in the zone between two worlds, the world of the living, and the world of the dying and the dead. My memory is that respect and calm hung heavily in the air – respect for a young man whose life had just come to an end, and respect for the terrible pain and shock his mother and father were now feeling. Within an hour, the tubes and machines had been taken away, and Ben was 'spruced up' as much as it is possible to be in those circumstances, and moved into a smaller, quieter room, where he lay in peace, under a white sheet, his shredded clothes (cut off him to get to his chest quickly) in a plastic bag on the floor.

We had already lost Ben when my brother Don arrived. Other

visitors were a Catholic priest from a nearby parish, who came in to minister the last rites (so short a ritual, and so terribly to the point), and two young policemen, whose job it was to take statements and to ask us to identify the body. The suddenness of Ben's death triggered this initial police involvement, as well as the autopsy and post-mortem which followed.

I have two pictures on my mobile phone from that night. They are both of Benjamin, and the file says that they were taken at 1.08 a.m. I took them because I wanted to capture – for myself, and anyone else interested in Ben's life – how peaceful Ben looked on the night we lost him. One part of me believes that I should include these pictures in this book. But another part of me is fearful about overly dramatising the worst moment of my life.

I have now seen and touched three dead people, all men: my grandfather, my father, and my son. My father looked like I thought he should look, except I was shocked at how cold he was, almost frozen, when I reached down to kiss him on the forehead on the morning of his funeral in the Catholic cathedral in Canberra. My grandfather was completely different. I hardly recognised him when I saw him a few hours after he had died; his face was racked and ravaged. There was no physical sign of peace to be found there, and yet he was a good man, my closest friend during my own childhood. I had to force myself to touch him, and I could do no more than lightly touch his forearm before recoiling back. My son was still warm, still himself, still wonderfully and completely his amazing self, when we said goodbye to him that night.

It was around 3 a.m. when we left Ben at the hospital that night. Esther and I both went back to my brother's house, near Morialta Falls in the Adelaide Hills, one of Ben's favourite places, and where he loved to feel the spray from the waterfall on his face. We sat with Don for a while, drinking tea and eating some muffins his wife Cathy had in the pantry. Esther and I then went for a long walk in the pre-dawn hours. It was finished. In the blink of an eye, our first child, our son, was gone. A long, long struggle had come to an end. We had lived with this dreadful knowledge for over twenty-one years; we had confronted many challenges, and succeeded with most of them; we had coped as best we could; we did our best; we had raised a son who was a fine human being and a man any parent would be proud to call their own. We had watched his terrible physical decline, but also the strength of spirit which never left him. But now, at this damp, cold, pre-dawn hour, surrounded by the dark and silent Australian bush, which Benjamin loved so much, it was finished.

> Once upon a time
> The world was sweeter than we knew
> Everything was ours
> How happy we were then
> But somehow once upon a time
> Never comes again

Whether it's Bobby Darin or even me singing these words, they are still true: the world was indeed sweeter than we knew when Benjamin was in the world and there was a smile on his face. I had seen that face smiling, laughing, grinning and chuckling many times. I had seen sadness too, and flashes of anger on rare occasions. What I never saw was a dark scowl, or any hate or bitterness. Not once. Yes, Benjamin's smile in the face of tough calls is his enduring legacy, his contribution to the human race, and to the meaning of the lives of those of us he lit up with that smile.

John O'Grady, the main character in Cormac McCarthy's *All the Pretty Horses*, gets a smile from strangers when he is down and out, and most in need of one. It is not a small thing. McCarthy writes about the power of a smile to protect, to confer honour, to strengthen resolve, to heal and spread goodwill.

Ben's smile was that kind of smile: noticed by all, to be talked about as long as anyone is alive who knew him well.

There is a gravel path leading from my carport to the front door. Ben would deliberately use the gravel drive just to get a rise out of me.

His wheelchair would leave deep ruts in the loose gravel, and more often than not he would get stuck (if he didn't keep up enough speed) and then I would have to pull the heavy chair out. For weeks after he had died, I would notice the ruts in the gravel, gradually filling in and disappearing. Now there is no sign that a wheelchair ever used that path. But for nearly a year I still stopped and looked, every week or so, even getting down on my hands and knees, trying to find some trace of his mark on the earth.

A fortnight after that night in the Emergency Department, Benjamin's obituary appeared in the *Adelaide Advertiser*:

Stoic and principled student
Benjamin Bede Galvin   Student, volunteer
Born: 13 November, 1984; Sydney
Died: 27 June, 2007; Adelaide

In the last week of his short life, Ben Galvin attended a UniSA symposium on the writings of war. He listened with particular interest to a talk about letters from wounded World War I servicemen; one had been written by a nurse on behalf of a paralysed soldier.

By this stage, at twenty-two, Ben himself needed help with his writing. He was learning a laptop voice recognition system as he intended to begin university studies. Over the years, Duchenne muscular dystrophy had gradually immobilised his limbs, also compromising his lung and heart function.

From the age of eleven, he had relied on an electric wheelchair for mobility. Ben accepted this stoically, as he accepted all facets of his condition. As his mother, Esther Caprez, recalls, 'All he said was, "I just miss feeling the ground under my feet"'.

But for some years afterwards, he could still swim, in both pool and ocean; he sailed solo in a modified dinghy; represented South Australia five times in wheelchair sport; carried the Olympic torch on its way through northern Adelaide; and played blackjack with dexterity and cunning.

That skill at the tables had its occasional reward, notably so in (very) early-morning sessions at the Adelaide Casino.

Born in Sydney, Ben had come to Adelaide in 1990 when his father, Dr Michael Galvin, took an academic post at the SA College of Advanced Education (now UniSA). He attended Mitcham Primary School and Unley High School, completing Year 12 with only one concession – writing his examinations on a laptop instead of by pen.

A multimedia certificate at TAFE followed, and then a WEA philosophy course, as a means of preparing for university entry in 2008. That hope had long been delayed, through the interruption of schooling by a spinal fusion and, later, by four bouts of pneumonia. Ben had found time, nevertheless, for data entry work as a volunteer at the Muscular Dystrophy Association.

He was a young man of strong principles, demonstrated in a refusal to use illicit software or to watch pirated DVDs and in his decision, in 2004, to join a street protest against hostilities in Iraq.

In less sober-sided commitments, Ben would manoeuvre his wired chariot into football stadiums and hard alongside the motor racing circuit fence – supporting, with a passion, the Crows in the AFL and Holden in the Clipsal 500.

Living at Glenelg, he loved to challenge the forces of the sea in winter when the waves smashed into the Esplanade. It was a race of electric wheelchair against water. If the waves won, interfering with the electronics, getting home became a further challenge.

Eighteen state sports squad teammates, in their wheelchairs, formed a guard of honour at his funeral.

His parents and his sister, Rosanna, spoke of Ben's dry sense of humour and his refined sense of irony. The congregation heard his Fatboy Slim and Cat Empire tracks, plus selected sound effects of his favourite high-performance motor vehicles.

And irony emerged as an enduring quality. For this ardent Holden petrolhead was conveyed to the chapel in a Ford Fairlane.

Author: Nigel Starck

(*The Adelaide Advertiser*, 10 July 2007. Reprinted with permission.)

Even now, when I reread this obituary, I am strangely troubled. There is no relief, no closure, in my friend's words. I cannot quite believe that I am reading the whole span of my son's life, summed up in six hundred words, from the first moment when he came slowly and reluctantly into the world until the last. It is indeed troubling. This complete span, from the alpha to the omega, eludes our experience most of the time. We do not get to experience our own lives like this, or our parents', or our children's, or our partners'. The thought that all of my son's potential, all of his possible futures, has always already been 'monumentalised' is almost unbearable to contemplate.

2

Paradise Lost

> Some natural tears they dropt, but wiped them soon:
> The world was all before them where to choose
> Their place of rest, and Providence their guide.
> They, hand in hand, with wand'ring steps and slow,
> Through Eden took their solitary way.

Thus concludes John Milton's epic tale of the fall of Adam and Eve, their banishment from the Garden of Eden and the beginnings of a new life, for them and for the rest of humankind. Even here, however, at their lowest ebb, all is not lost. The tears flow, but they dry up soon enough. The world is all before them, and is still full of choices, full of possibilities. They still have human touch; flowers still bloom; beautiful sunsets and cloudy skies come and go. They can still move on, albeit slowly, falteringly, and prone to errors of one kind or another.

From the moment that Benji, aged fourteen months, was diagnosed with Duchenne muscular dystrophy in January 1986, I found myself in the same ambivalent place that Milton describes here.

Overall, I have been spared many heart-stopping moments, moments when you know with dreadful certainty that one period of your life has irrevocably ended and a different one has begun. The moment of marriage breakdown in 2004 was one such moment; the moment of Ben's death in 2007 was another. The 1986 moment I am writing about here was the first. In each case, a paradise of sorts was lost. In each case, a new world had to be found, a world still capable of some delight, despite soul-destroying loss, regret and foreboding.

It is January 1986, and we have just arrived back in Sydney from a holiday in Tasmania. What I thought was to be a routine visit to a paediatrician was in the diary for the next day. I didn't give a second's thought to that approaching doctor's appointment at any time while in Tasmania. Benji was a delightful, placid baby boy. From day one, he had been a peaceful and calm baby. However, despite appearing normal in every way, an alert community nurse at the local child care centre had noted what was not obvious to his parents or anyone else – that he was just a little bit slower than normal in his physical development – and had recommended some routine blood tests a month earlier.

I remember answering the phone an hour or so after getting back from the airport. It was the doctor's secretary, ringing to confirm that we had not forgotten the appointment, and wanting to make doubly sure that we were going to keep it. As I put the phone down, it struck me even then that such a phone call was a little out of the ordinary. It made complete sense to me twenty-four hours later. The doctor knew the news that he was to deliver: that the results of the routine blood test pointed to the high likelihood that Benji had Duchenne muscular dystrophy (DMD). The first question he would have seen coming from the stunned mother and father sitting in front of him, a little boy on their knees: muscular dystrophy – what on earth is that? Surely there must be some mistake?

(Now, many years later, those few minutes just before the announcement that changed everything have also stayed with me. I understand that trauma etches itself into the brain; but does it also work retrospectively? Freezing in time the 'just before', the last moments of normalcy, as well as the shock itself? Sitting, relaxed, in the waiting room for the doctor that morning, those last minutes are as vivid as the diagnosis moment itself.)

We stumbled out of his office. Fifteen minutes earlier, we had been watching Benji playing on the floor with the toys in the waiting room. Now a whole series of medical wheels had been set in motion, in tandem with the knowledge not only that he had just been given a fatal prognosis, but that a life of wheelchairs and other unimagined challenges lay ahead for him, and for us.

It was a couple of weeks before I was able to face my colleagues at work. My boss came into my office on my first day back, and did his best to console me with some of the sadnesses that had happened when he was a young father. Leaning forward in my chair while he talked, unable to look him in the eye, a slow drip of tears formed a tiny wet patch near my shoes on the office carpet.

Before that day back on campus, much had happened. Benji had been operated on; muscle tissue had been taken out of his arm and leg (the post-mortem in Adelaide twenty-one years later noted the old scar on his left arm but not the one on his left thigh); the results had proven conclusive for DMD; a new world order had begun. The muscle biopsy operation took place in the Children's Hospital at Randwick, NSW. That particular hot summer afternoon seemed as if it would never end. The western sun shone fiercely through the curtains of the infants' ward. The specialist was Dr Graeme Morgan, a man who had devoted most of his professional life to those with this disease. Dr Morgan came into the ward to see us just as Benji was waking up from the anaesthetic. Apart from confirming the grim diagnosis, he said little. But he spent a long, long time, at least an hour, with us, just standing there, next to Benji's cot.

Dr Morgan reminds me now of the way T.S. Eliot describes the figure of Tiresias:

> I Tiresias, old man with wrinkled dugs
> Perceived the scene, and foretold the rest –
> (And I Tiresias have foresuffered all
> Enacted on this same divan or bed;
> I who have sat by Thebes below the wall
> And walked among the lowest of the dead.)

I have often wondered how a busy specialist holding a senior position in a major hospital would or could choose to spend so long with us that day, as if there was nothing else on his mind except this apparently normal little boy starting to stir in his hospital cot. I think I understand it better now, having lived through Benjamin's life cycle from beginning to end, and feeling like Tiresias myself when I meet newly diagnosed young boys for the first time. Dr Morgan knew the full span of Benji's life-to-be, and he knew our future too. He had perceived and foresuffered this scene many times before, and could foretell the rest. Compared to him, we knew nothing about what life now had in store for us. He stood there with us for so long, because this fearful knowledge weighed on his shoulders, weighed him down. A dreadful truth had been confirmed, including the death of a dream about a happy and normal future for this family. In the face of such knowledge, what humane and honourable man would not just stand there for a time, in silent solidarity with a mother and father who are still too shocked to be fully grief-stricken?

*

On page 200 of my 1975 Masters thesis, there is a quote from an E.M. Forster novel:

> One must behave as if one is immortal, and as if civilisation is eternal. Both statements are false – I shall not survive, no more will the great globe itself – both of them must be assumed to be true if we are to go on eating and working and travelling, and keep open a few breathing holes for the human spirit.

This focus on 'as if' as a philosophy of life resonated with me as an immature young man. It crops up again in four words from Forster's *A Room With a View* incorporated into my thesis title:

> The 'transitory Yes' and 'everlasting Why': narrative methods and philosophical theme in the early novels of E.M. Forster

My 'Yes' is damaged and dimmer these days, a votive candle in a church rather than a busy, unruly sun in the cosmos; as for the 'Why', it just keeps on getting bigger and blacker. It was an easy, self-indulgent choice when I was twenty and knew nothing about anything. Not such an easy, choice, perhaps, for Ben when he was twenty and knowing he was in the final years of his life. Whatever. The exact quote in the novel goes as follows

> Then make my boy think like us. Make him realise that by the side of the Everlasting why there is a Yes – a transitory Yes if you like, but a Yes.

I don't know the extent to which I somehow made my boy think like me or think like this. But I do know this: he lived his life as if he would live forever, fearlessly and fully, as if the sensory surprises and pleasures of nature would never end. Benjamin enjoyed being alive, he delighted in the exhilaration of being. It was true when he was two years old, and it was just as true when he was twenty-two.

This extraordinary natural world that we live in was Benjamin's natural world too. His mother in particular gave him this deep, abiding, love and delight in nature. She gave him the ability to be thrilled by the way that nature can be an endless adventure playground. (My take on nature was much less adventurous: sitting by a campfire in the Australian bush, a gum leaf or two in the billy, a sense of peace, isolation and comfort that came from being out in the bush, not any bush, but the Australian bush, yarning while staring at the flames licking the logs and sending sparks into the cold, night air.) Yes, his mother gave Ben his delight in earth, fire, water and air, in all their myriad combinations.

He was weeks rather than months old when he was lying on a blanket at Caves Beach, in Jervis Bay, his hanging toy above him attached to the top of a Yalumba cardboard wine cask, the grey ashes of a nearby bushfire floating gently down onto his baby clothes at this idyllic, isolated beach. Ten years later, and we are again sitting on this same beach, while Benji and his sister are playing in the sand about twenty metres away. We look up to see both of them being washed like seaweed up the beach by a rogue wave. A frantic race to grab them from the swirling foam before the wave starts to recede back into the ocean. Rosanna and I are terrified; Benji and his mother laugh and laugh with the thrill of it all.

Ben went on dozens of camping trips with Rosanna and his parents. As his physical impairments became more serious, camping became more challenging, before it eventually became impossible. When it became too difficult to deal with him on the floor of the tent, we bought a camp bed, and he slept on that. When his legs became too 'distended' to fit into a regular sleeping bag, we improvised with doonas and blankets. One winter's night, we were camped near the Murray River in South Australia. Waking up in the morning, we realised that Benji had spent part of the sub-zero night with one bare leg sticking out from under the blankets.

Why didn't you say something, Ben? It was freezing. There was frost on the ground, even if it looked just like the salt more common in those parts. Let me guess. You didn't want any of us to have to face the fact that camping trips were becoming too difficult for us to cope with any more. Am I right?

Yes, Ben's love affair with nature began well before he reached conscious awareness, and never ended. When he could indulge no more, he observed and watched. Instead of feeling the sand beneath his feet, he would imagine what it was like to feel the sand beneath his feet. He had to notice things. Five days before he died, he took me outside my house, to show me the exact spot in my backyard where the sun's rays retreated to on the shortest day of the year. He was interested in tiny details like that. Once, at Bondi Beach, he had to stay with me on the concrete esplanade while his mum and sister went for a swim. He enjoyed the surf through them. That they got pleasure gave him pleasure. Most of the time, anyway. Those times when his own disappointment took over were rare, fortunately so for me, because his naked pain when it broke through the surface of his equanimity was frightening in its rawness and reality.

For several years, Ben looked forward to our Saturday morning trips to the Blackwood farm in the Adelaide Hills, where he joined in the Riding for the Disabled program. We both liked this feeling of arriving on a working farm, the smell of the animals, the fresh sunny mornings, the Hans Heysen gums along the road, the satisfaction we both got when and while he was on the horse. Slowly but surely, it became more and more difficult, and eventually impossible, to get him on a horse. For the record, let it be noted that he never fell off a horse (a fact which now astounds me), even though he had a few run-ins with other animals.

*

Tall tales? The rooster, the goat and the emu

'And do you know something, kids, this really happened, many years ago. Would I tell a fib to you? Would I exaggerate or make things up? It was a mild and cloudy evening, in the hills about fifty kilometres north-west of Melbourne, in the year of the rooster. Legend has it that roosters, especially Chinese roosters, are more cocky than ever at that time. This rooster was so full of himself, I swear he was at least twice as big as he normally is. He was so cocky, he would strut up to a cow, and the cow would give way. Maybe I shouldn't have told you, Benji, about this enormous rooster, prowling and pecking and strutting its way around the farm like a maharajah, but I did. What's done is done. We adults were sitting on the veranda, a cold beer or a glass of wine in hand, with no greater care in the world than making sure there was enough gas in the barbie for the marinated prawns and duck and veal sausages.

Anyway, Benji, you were curious. You believed your dad, especially when he told you tall stories. You just had to see this rooster for yourself. We adults continued to chat while you slowly made your way to the rooster's turf in chookland about fifty metres away.

With one almighty leap, the rooster hurls itself into the air, wings flapping, and lands a direct blow on your arm. More rooster cursing, and then a direct blow from the sharp, shiny spurs to your back. Feathers and dust everywhere. You go down. The raging rooster, in a frenzy more likely to be seen in a Balinese cockfight, pecks and kicks at your white Chesty Bond singlet. We run over, the rooster retreats, and we find you lying in the farmyard dust, dazed. Your Chesty Bond has been shredded, there are bits of white cotton and red spots where there are scratches. That night, you didn't want to take that singlet off, you were so proud of your war wounds from this clash with the rooster dragon.

Well, yes, this is a bit of a tall tale. But I used to tell my kids tall tales all the time when they were young and eager to believe. And Benji did come off second best after he was attacked by a rooster, just like the story says.

And this story is also true, with hardly a word of exaggeration. Benji is nearly ten years old, and we are staying in an old derelict caravan at Cudlee Creek in the Adelaide Hills. That old caravan full of spiders disappeared into history a few years later, when it was washed away by a flash flood. Maybe it ended up in the Torrens Lake in the centre of Adelaide? Anyway, we are at a local children's zoo, when a feisty old goat comes right up to Benji. Our boy at first tries the Crocodile Dundee defence, attempting to stare down the goat, thereby immobilising the wild beast. It doesn't work. The stand-off seems to go on forever, but then it ends. The goat snorts, charges, and head butts him in the chest, sending Benji flying through the air. For a moment or two, he looked like a Warner Brothers cartoon character, in suspended animation, hurtling through space.

Ben's interest in animals was as deep-seated for him as it was problematic for his anxious parents. He was never strong or stable enough when he was on his feet for us to be able to relax when animals were around. It also didn't help that he had no fear of most animals, spiders and sharks excepted. Animal management for us morphed into constant risk management.

Managing animal risk reached its climax on a trip we went on soon after he started using an electric wheelchair. We were in the Glenelg River Park, a stunning area near the South Australian/Victorian border, not far from the sea. We had gone for a long walk on a loop trail only just wide enough for a wheelchair. We had almost completed the six-kilometre walk, and the car park and our van were in sight about a hundred metres away. But right in front of us, unmoving on the trail, was an emu standing over her brood of tiny youngsters. As the minutes wore on, our initial delight at seeing such amazing wildlife slowly turned to apprehension. The emu did not seem to have the slightest intention of vacating the path for us. What to do? We could try and walk up to her, hoping she would move off on her own accord. But what if she got aggressive and defensive? What if she pecked Ben in his chair? He was defenceless, unable to lift his arms to protect his eyes or other parts of his body. What if blindness was added to his other afflictions?

We were tired. His battery was running out of charge. But we couldn't risk any such injury to him, and so we did the whole walk again in reverse, retracing our steps. The emu was still there when we arrived at the other end of the track, hardly visible because by now it was already quite dark.

Yes, Ben loved all four of the natural elements: earth, water, fire and air. As his ability to actually engage with nature decreased, it seemed that his powers of natural observation became more intense. King tides were a favourite, especially in winter. Their times would be noted in his well-thumbed copy of the *South Australian Almanac*, and, if there was a storm as well, we would go down to the shore at Glenelg to see the waves at their height crashing over the rocky breakwater, and foamy water flow onto and up the Broadway, sometimes for a hundred metres or more.

He loved every aspect of storms – the wind, rain, hail, the effects on land and sea. He loved to see the leaves and branches lying on the ground after a storm had passed. For my fiftieth birthday, he gave me a signed, framed and laminated copy of a poem he had written about the effects of a storm in our backyard. It is called 'Aftermath'.

> Cool breeze ruffles
> through the leaves
> light spreads through
> the tree tops
> lying twigs are strewn
> across the dirt
> like ripples in a
> calm sea
> plus leaves on ground
> making it look like
> bomb has hit
> shaking the leaves off.
> A light layer of clouds
> with little bits of blue
> poking out making the
> situation calm.
> A big difference from
> 24 hours ago.

On the bottom is written in his own shaky hand, 'Benjamin, for your 50th Birthday'.

It seemed that the happy routine of our family life, lived so much of the time in direct relation to each of the four seasons and the four elements, would go on forever, but of course it couldn't and it didn't; it went on like this for about ten years.

The following words appeared in the *Australian* newspaper the day after the funeral for Glenn McGrath's wife, Jane, took place in Sydney:

> For years Glenn had a stock answer to enquiries about life at home: 'Never been better, mate, never been better.'
> Though many suspected trying times, he always seemed to believe the words. (26 June 2008, p. 3)

Glenn McGrath was Ben's kind of Australian cricketer, and these words are exactly what Ben would have said throughout his childhood, and what I would have said a lot of the time too. We had our own paradise on earth for a time. Despite everything, despite the wheelchair and all it stood for, we were together as a family, we knew who we were, and we were happy. And this was never more the case than around the time of my fiftieth birthday in 1998, when we went on a houseboat trip on the River Murray with close family friends.

A ritual instantly formed around the evening moorings. We would pull up on some part of the river where it was reasonably safe for Ben to drive down the ramp onto the river bank in his wheelchair. It felt like the middle of nowhere, but was in fact only a few kilometres from the Sturt Highway. There were four kids, including Ben. Insofar as some fathers tend to be older kids themselves when they are around children, with similar pyromaniac tendencies, so it was us two dads and the kids out gathering up fallen branches from gum trees (those with lots of dead leaves still attached especially prized) and long, dry reeds and rushes from the river's edge. The branches and reeds were loaded onto Ben's wheelchair, and he would lead us in pagan procession to the chosen site for that evening's bonfire. It could have been a scene out of *Lord of the Flies*, except it wasn't, it was the complete opposite. By the second night it had a name – 'the ceremony of the leaves' – and each night the anticipation became more intense, the bonfire got bigger and higher, as we became more and more daring. Ben would be the one urging us on, wanting to make it more and more exciting.

Life couldn't have been better, mate. A frosty winter's night on Australia's greatest river, with friends and family intact, and exploding leaves bursting like firecrackers, sending thousands of sparks into the night sky, momentarily obscuring the Milky Way and Southern Cross above us. A boy in a wheelchair roaming over the dark landscape, for the moment completely happy in his own skin, and in the world we shared.

Most of Benjamin's childhood was like this. Yet after the events of more recent years, I so easily forget. In a low mood a few months ago, I tentatively asked my daughter whether she remembered any happy times from her childhood. 'I only remember happy times,' she shot back at me. True, yes, up to a point. Also true that a two-year-old girl mangling the words 'muscular dystrophy' (before she could say these words, and before she even knew many other words) points to the shadow that also lay at the heart of our family life. Sitting around a campfire or a bonfire, it was as if we were all so drawn in by the warmth and comfort of the flames, that we could put off indefinitely thinking about the cold shadows just outside our comfort zone, our circle of warmth and light.

Family photo

I am looking at a family photograph that stood in the kitchen in our Glenelg home for many years. For some reason, it came to me in the messy and painful division of ordinary worldly possessions that a marriage break-up entails. It had gathered so much grease and grime over the years that it took several cleans before it went back up on the mantel place in my lounge room.

In this photo, Rosanna is a chubby one-year-old baby, with no hair, but rings of baby fat from neck to toe that got her the nickname, the Michelin baby. Benji, two years older, also appears to be without bathers. Leaning confidently towards the camera, his skin is brown, his blond hair wet, his white teeth clearly visible. He has an absolutely typical Benjamin smile on his face. This picture of him naked reminds me of when he was a baby. I had the task of washing him in a tub in our bathroom. I remember that I used to say to him, 'What a beautiful baby boy you are.' There was not the slightest thing about how he looked then to predict what was going to happen to his body. But perhaps I must have already sensed this, to remember so vividly that I used to think such things at all. Otherwise, such sentimental self-talk would have been ridiculous.

Although he is a couple of years older in this backyard family photograph, there is still not the slightest sign that he is going to spend over half his twenty-two years in a wheelchair. Both kids are sitting in a green clamshell pool, the water about ten centimetres deep, Esther in with them, wearing a one-piece swimsuit that she looked very good in.

She looks young. As the writer Joan Didion noted about herself, she always thought of herself as a thirty-four-year-old because that is the age she was in her husband's eyes, the age she was when he met and married her. When he died nearly forty years later, she felt herself suddenly aged, suddenly a lifetime older. I cannot imagine that Esther will ever look old to me, for similar reasons.

I am sitting behind them, one bare foot on the edge of the kiddie pool, one hand holding a beer stubby. I am wearing a wide straw hat, a loose, white, Chinese coolie-style T-shirt (a mild affectation of mine at the time) and khaki shorts. Behind me it is apparent from the luxuriant green vines cascading down that the pumpkin seeds I planted are thriving. A red brick parapet is partly visible. I planted tomatoes and capsicums in the natural garden bed that this brick wall created, and used to lift both kids onto the top row of bricks so they could see the little seedlings growing into different vegetables.

A moment frozen in time. Let's call it 5 p.m., on 31 January 1988. We had lived in this bland suburban house in the Blue Mountains west of Sydney for about a year, and had about another year to go before we moved into a place where we really wanted to live. Esther, thirty-six years old, looks happy enough, although I know she never liked living in this bland, God-fearing, prim and proper neighbourhood. Rosanna has that look of mild concern that never left her while her brother was alive and 'at risk' from forces that she could not comprehend, but picked up instinctively from her parents. I look the most contented of all, and I probably was. I was thirty-nine years old, living in what I considered a beautiful natural environment, I had exactly the kind of academic job that I had studied long and hard for, and I was providing for my family. The idea (and satisfaction) of protecting my family from any threats that might befall them was uppermost in my mind, in a self-validating kind of way. Muscular dystrophy was a black cloud that was not going to become a hurricane or even a storm for a few more years, at least; in the meantime, I had this perfect family life (just look at the picture), and no end to it seemed in sight. I did support and protect them – for a long time – but the day did come when there was nothing I could do to save my own son, and the idea of staying a 'normal' family became an impossibility.

Decades later, I am holding and studying that photo. Apart from the fact that I am still close to my daughter, nothing is left of that family unit. Is there anything to learn? What can I learn? For one thing, this photo appears to capture all four of us in the exact same moment in time. Benji and Rosanna are together, and will be together and forever this exact age in this photograph, not a day older and not a day younger; Esther and I will be forever at the prime of our lives – the loving and doting parents that we were. Yet what strikes me as I write is the illusion that this photo aids and abets. I remember enough of those days to recall that at the time they felt like they would go on forever, that the familiar routines of caring for these kids would go on, more or less like this, indefinitely. No end was in sight, or even imaginable. There was not much meaningful past and no plausible future. All energy went on this eternal present, the present of raising a young family. Change from day to day seemed infinitesimal and illusory.

The second thing that strikes me is less obvious. Four people are in this picture. They look like they are in the same reality, or even are the same reality, but they are not. They share the three dimensions of space, and appear to share a fourth – time – except they don't. Just as the stars appear to be glued to their fixed positions in relation to each other at any given moment, but are not, the four people in this picture are speeding through the universe at different speeds and in different directions. The nuclear family is not frozen (as in this frame) but is itself a constant nuclear reaction.

Benjamin was speeding through this universe several times faster than his sister. He had already lived over 15% of his life when this picture was taken, when he was three years old; she had lived through less than 4% of hers if she had only lived as long as her brother, and less than 1% if she lives to the age of her grandmother. Though it is not obvious, those two kids were speeding along at a rate that made their parents look like stone statues in comparison. Parents, once reaching cruising altitude in their middle years, may not change much from one decade to the next; their children, however, go through epochs of change in any given decade you can think of: from birth to ten, or ten to twenty, or five to fifteen, or any other ten-year span in that range.

Family photographs. What Zygmund Bauman says about individual identity also applies to family identity, when captured at moments like these:

> Identities seem fixed and stable only when seen, in a flash, from outside. Whatever solidity they might have when contemplated from the inside of one's own biographical experience appears fragile, vulnerable, and constantly torn apart by shearing forces which lay bare its fluidity and by cross-currents which threaten to rend in pieces and carry away any form they might have acquired... The experienced, lived identity could only be held together with the adhesive of fantasy, perhaps day-dreaming. Yet, given the stubborn evidence of biographical experience, any stronger glue – a substance with more fixing power than easy-to-dissolve-and-wipe-out fantasy – would seem as repugnant a prospect as the absence of day dreams. (Bauman, *Liquid Modernity*, p. 83)

Substitute 'family' for 'identities' in this passage from Bauman, and you have a fair description of what I see when I now look at this photograph of when my children were very young. We were in a dream, held together with the adhesive of fantasy, such a dream that it hardly makes sense that any third party could even be in this private space to take the photograph at all. Who that interloper was, I have no memory. Even Adam and Eve went on to have a family. They too had their paradise on earth, at least while their offspring were small.

3

Beach Scenes From the 1950s

It is getting late on a clear, cold Sunday afternoon in August 1989. At first they appear as little specks in the sky, like gnats in the air during a backyard barbecue. Then their lights become visible. Slowly these glowing dots become aeroplanes, most of them with red kangaroos on their tails. One by one, they fly in over a roiling blue sea, a deep golden sunset behind them. By the time they pass from left to right across my field of vision, they are low, slow-moving, glistening machines just a few seconds from touchdown at Adelaide Airport.

For the first time ever, we are on the Esplanade at Glenelg, a few metres from the jetty, looking out to sea, eating fish and chips. We have come to this tourist spot on our first trip to Adelaide, largely because it is a tourist spot. I have never heard of Glenelg before. We were in Adelaide for a job interview for me. During the flight, the pilot has allowed four-year-old Benji into the cockpit – a thrill for any boy before 9/11 changed so many things.

I took the job, and we made the big move to Adelaide. A family friend offered to find a house for us to rent, the house was in Glenelg, we liked what we had seen a few months earlier, and so it was that by January 1990, we found ourselves living in a pleasant, seaside suburb that we had never heard of six months before.

Eighteen years later, it is May 2008, and I am in Glenelg again, this time to see my doctor, the same quiet young fellow who was also Ben's GP, and one who Ben felt very comfortable with for reasons not obvious to the rest of us. The same doctor who was eventually sent

Ben's final medical results – the post-mortem report. It is a beautiful morning, the air is fresh, and the sea is glistening only a short walk away. I am halfway through writing this story about Benjamin but, until now, Glenelg has not figured very prominently in my writing or thinking. A thousand feelings and memories suddenly flash in my face on this bright, sunny morning, and I know there must be a chapter about Glenelg if what I write is even going to scratch the surface of who and what Ben was.

Ben lived in Glenelg from 1990 to 2006 – for sixteen of his twenty-two years. Even though he travelled out of the area every day to go to school, he was a Glenelg boy through and through, a product of a beachside surf culture far more than anyone else in the family. Whenever it was warm enough, we went to the beach for a swim, and when it wasn't warm enough, we went to the beach to walk along the sea shore. Ben was always the keenest to go. He would play with his sister in the sand and in the water in front of the old cement-block kiosk at Glenelg South, where the Broadway meets the coast. Not once or twice, but hundreds of times. Even when we didn't feel like it, we still made the effort, because we knew that his opportunities to enjoy surf and sand were going to end before long.

Both kids had boogie boards, and played with them for hours. Except for storms (more common in winter than summer), the waves were mostly gentle, just right for someone with Benji's strength to get a ride and not be thrown about too much. For years, he was able to ride the wave in, end up on the sand, slowly get himself back up on his feet (by 'walking' his hands up his legs, as many boys with his disease do), and struggle back out again with his blue boogie board.

We kept going to the beach, long after the boogie boards had been put away, two more pieces of redundant family memorabilia stored in a termite-infested garage. But I can still see him riding those waves, his blue board underneath him, holding onto it for grim life, and with a huge, thrilled grin on his face, smiling from ear to ear, white teeth glistening in the sun.

Watching Benji and Rosanna play in the sand was an exercise in observing two completely different personalities at work. When it was time to go home, Rosanna would always have something to show for her efforts (a castle or a racing track or something), but Benjamin would only have a few shapeless piles of sand, signifying little except some grand plan in his own mind. He was a perfectionist, always seeking to improve on what he had just done. The result was that he was nearly always in the demolition/start again phase.

He loved the beach: the sand, the water, the wind, the sun. He trusted us completely to protect him. I don't think he ever had a moment's fear in the water, except for sharks. The shark phobia was no doubt my doing: I would pretend to be a shark and come up behind him and his sister underwater and scare them. I enjoyed seeing my kids love the beach, and get so much of it in their childhoods but, if I am honest, I never enjoyed it that much myself. For one thing, the days were generally too hot if they were not too cold. On days when it was really hot, it was usually too hot to go out of doors at all. And on such hot days, the dry wind would generally be blowing from the north, from the desert, blowing brackish seawater south towards Adelaide's beaches from further up the gulf, water which felt itchier and slimier than when it was really cold.

Glenelg might be a poor substitute for a decent Australian beach like Bondi or Manly. Only South Australians would think otherwise. But Glenelg, and particularly South Glenelg, more through accident than design, became our beach, and especially our children's beach, even if the sand had to be trucked in to cover the rocky, murky bottom near the waterline and the prevailing wind was a cold south-westerly that blew in from the Southern Ocean. And Benjamin really, really loved this bit of beach and the Australian surfie culture it signified in its own modest way.

Once wheelchair-bound, and before his lifestyle was even more controlled by the weather, Ben would lead the rest of us again and again on trips to the paved Esplanade. The nine-hundred-metre walk from our house in Partridge Street down Broadway to the beach, then nine hundred metres along the Esplanade to Jetty Road, and back again, was our most common afternoon outing for ten years. When it was high tide, Benjamin would drive down one of the steep concrete ramps onto the sand (so steep we would have to hold on to stop the chair skidding down and into the sea), and go as far as he dared towards the edge, waiting for the next wave to come towards the ramp. The only way he would stay clear was to back up very quickly. It gave him a thrill even if it gave us a pounding heart to watch this little game of chicken with the waves. He loved water, and waves in water, and the spray that comes when wave and water meet rock. He loved the element of risk. He loved getting drenched, even when it was a foolhardy thing to do.

For years after it had become impossible for him to get into the sea on his own, we used a thing known as a platypus, a water-friendly plastic wheelchair with big wide wheels that could be pushed (with difficulty) across sand, and into the water. Ben would remain strapped in until we were about waist-deep. Then we would undo the strap and tip him out. Without both of us there to right him, he would have drowned every time, as his body weight was such as to keep him upside down in the water. Trust. He knew the chances of drowning in the company of his parents was zero. Getting him out of the water reminded me of watching the space shuttle dock with the space station. Line his bum up with the chair. Watch the waves. Go with the flow. Contact. Snap. Belt clipped around his cold, clammy tummy to hold him in the platypus. Pull him and the chair out across the sand. Once. Twice. Fifty, a hundred times. Dry him as quickly as possible to warm him up. Repeat a fairly similar physically demanding process transferring him into his electric wheelchair to get him back home. Another day at the beach.

How do you remain the cheerful, adventure-loving, pun-addicted, risk-taking, nature lover you are, and have to be handled so much of the time as if you have no more purpose or intentions or feelings or brains than a sack of potatoes? I don't know. But Ben could, and Ben did.

Moving into Glenelg in 1990 felt like moving into a land that time forgot, a step back into the 1950s. The only portent of the gross redevelopment that would be fully underway before the decade was out was the half-completed Grand Hotel, at a prime location at the tram terminus on the waterfront. A lot of the area that is now taken over by expensive apartment blocks was a mix of windswept vacant space, down at heel amusement parks, and poorly maintained bituminised carparks. Glenelg seemed at ease with its identity as an Aussie Blackpool or Coney Island, unaware that it would soon be developing Surfers Paradise pretensions of its own. It was still possible for a single mum we knew to buy an apartment unit with sea views, on an income not much more than the pension, even though her kids had the bedrooms and she slept in the kitchen. For years, it seemed as if there were always apartments within walking distance of the beach on sale for less than $100,000. It was still possible to buy a hammer or a nail at a suburban hardware shop on Jetty Road. There were still real shops like that on Jetty Road, not just cafés, restaurants and businesses aimed at tourists and day trippers. Cafés still sold milkshakes, not a dozen varieties of macchiato. You didn't have to be a barista to work in them.

Part of me was aware at the time that I was moving into some kind of time warp, and that I was attracted to and liked that feeling more than I knew I should. I now think that I was taking refuge in a world of nostalgia, in an idealised world of a previous era, where the man went out to work, to provide for his wife and children, where the woman willingly spent most of her time raising the children and maintaining the house, and where both parents found satisfaction inside this tight nuclear family. It was an impossible scenario decades earlier, and structurally unstable and deeply flawed when I lived it out too, an accidental anachronism in my particular case, but it provided me with a zone of refuge from what lay outside this comfort zone – all the terrors and foreboding that I felt about what was going to happen to Benjamin, and therefore the rest of us. Inside our cosy house, the wind and rain was kept out, and we could also forget for a time about the huge, unspoken Damocles sword that was hanging over 104 Partridge Street, Glenelg. It was as if we could pretend it didn't exist up there just above the roof line if we didn't talk about it. If I had started to hold my breath in 1986 when Benji was diagnosed with muscular dystrophy, I was still holding it for most of the 1990s, even if I was starting to turn ever darker shades of blue.

In his book about growing up, Barack Obama reflects on the ambiguity inherent in writing about our own past. He is pondering on what the civil rights television documentaries of his childhood meant for him later in life. He is acutely conscious that what he remembers about those childhod experiences bears a vexed relationship not only with what he might have thought at the time, but with what he subsequently creates in his own mind from such 'memories'.

Obama succinctly describes the double relationship my writing now has with what it is about. In the past, I had experiences; in the past, I also formed constructs that gave meaning to those experiences. Now, at the time of writing, I cannot be exactly sure of the relationship between these two things – the experiences, and when and how I attached meanings to them. How congruent were they? I don't know. Maybe the constructs kept forming just when I needed them, to give enough meaning to the past, to what had been going on, to enable me to have enough faith and strength to face the future.

But what I am sure of is that I loved being the breadwinner for my family, and I loved those times when my children were young. For most of that time, I worked as a department head in a university, and my days were full of intense, frequently vitriolic, but usually petty crises. I loved that feeling of arriving home, putting a key in the front door, and hearing my two children shout 'Daddy, Daddy' as they came to greet me, seemingly overjoyed that I was home; Rosanna arriving at the door first because she could run, and then Benji walking awkwardly behind, and both of them grabbing hold of one of my legs each, and carrying on like crazed dervishes.

I shall remember this moment. The silence, the twilight, the bowls of strawberries and milk, your faces in the evening light… I'll try to remember what we talked about. I'll carry this memory between my hands as carefully as if it were a bowl filled to the brim with fresh milk… And it will be an adequate sign – it will be enough for me. (*Seventh Seal* screenplay)

From time to time during my happy years in Glenelg, this scene from *The Seventh Seal* – a classic film from my student days – would come to mind. In my version of the Knight's relentless and doomed game of chess with Death, I also had a sign, and it was enough for me: being greeted by my two young children at the front door when I arrived home from work. Those happy family days, when my children were little, are long since over, finished, extinct, nothing but flawed, fading memories. But I knew something important at the time, and I know it now. It was enough for me; enough then and enough now. My bowl overflowed with strawberries, and milk too. I was the luckiest and happiest man alive. It was as if all my life I had been preparing for this main role, as father and protector, and now I was at ease on that stage and happy in my own skin.

It's a strange feeling – when big chunks of your life feel like they are nothing but preparation for something, for some main event. I felt this way during many of the years leading up to being a father of young children, even though I had done nothing remotely 'fatherlike' up to that point. Maybe it is not so strange. A clue comes from the occasional sensation I had when speaking with my kids at certain times, like when they were in bed and I was saying good night to them, or when I was wandering aimlessly around the house whistling mainly to myself. It wasn't me there, I wasn't there at all, it was my father's voice, he was standing just behind me. My father was gone by then; he had died a few years after we moved to South Australia. Somehow, I had grown into who my father was when I was a young child. The point? My life as a son was covert preparation for when I became a father. I also had this same feeling sometimes about Ben – that he was somehow becoming me, even though the opposite made no sense at all.

Nevertheless, I never did manage to convince him to take an interest in films like *The Seventh Seal*, although I note here that Ben developed a fascination with the films of John Malkovitch – to the point of purchasing a poster for the *Ripley* movie he starred in. But he did become a chess enthusiast for a time, while he had the strength to move the pieces on the board.

In front of me I have a little trophy. Inscribed under the mounted king:

> B. Galvin   1st Place
> Div. 2   Chess Club   April 1998

Living in Glenelg, the weeks became months, the months years, and the years more than a decade. I was living the suburban dream – in a middle-class house, in a salubrious suburb, with a middle-class wife, and two middle-class children – but nevertheless not quite able to feel authentically middle class myself. While I felt satisfied that I had 'made it', I also felt unease, a feeling that I was mainly lucky, and that what I now had could easily be taken away again. It was as if, just above the roof, just above the television aerial, there were gremlins and witches on broomsticks in the sky and, if I was not careful, they would come swooping down and scare the hell out of me. I loved what I had in Glenelg, but never felt completely at home there. It seemed too good to be true. It *was* too good to be true.

In the back of my mind, I had never forgotten Max Gillies playing Monk O'Neill twenty years earlier. Monk, eking out his days in some godforsaken backblock of Victoria, dining with ants, growing the odd tomato, talking to his dead dog, reminding his deceased mate Mort of the time he told Les Darcy to get real and stop trying to extract sunbeams from cucumbers. Maybe what happens to Monk, after his days of wine, women and song, is what happens to Catholic boys with a good classics education? Maybe it was my fate too? It would have seemed like self-indulgent posturing if I had said as much during the good Glenelg years. A few years later, the analogy did not seem quite so far-fetched.

Slowly but surely, clear signs that we could not control our world, and that I could not protect or save Benji (or any of us, for that matter), began to find their way into our castle – clear proof that we were not living in a timeless idyllic land where it was always going to be morning in paradise, but living in the real world, a world of change, an entropic, dystrophic world.

For a while, Benji's room was a normal boy's bedroom, with a giant poster of Shane Warne and other Australian cricketers on one wall, pictures of Holden cars on another, a galaxy of fluorescent stars stuck onto the ceiling, slowly turning into the Milky Way when the lights went out. But things slowly changed. Ramps, when single steps became too difficult for him to step up. A manual wheelchair, when he became too tired to walk, and on it went, until, after a decade or so, his bedroom had slowly lost the feel of a teenage boy's own room, and had become more of a control room, a manual handling warehouse. Electric wheelchair, charger, hoist, sling, hoist charger, shower chair, electric bed, bi-pap machine, emergency battery in case of black outs, power boards to the left, power boards to the right. Aliens had invaded the house, and taken it and us over. The outside world that we had somehow kept at bay for a long time, for most of the 1990s, had come right in and become the hosts. We were now totally dependent on these machines and such stuff for any semblance of a normal life.

Meanwhile, Benji, the human metronome, went to and from school each day, chuckled over my bad jokes at the dinner table, played *Mario*, enjoyed his favourite TV programs. Carers were now coming to shower and toilet him in the evenings. It was a routine that went on and on, our paths crossing only briefly on schooldays, the routines so rigid and unchanging that they could have been set in concrete. If it was Sunday night, it was a cheese omelette, Spanish-style, with onion and potato; if it was Friday, it was *pepperoni al fucho* from the local pizza shop (Benji enjoyed the way I twisted and stressed the word '*fucho*' – 'ch' sounds like 'k', right? – on the phone to the pizza man, not once, not twice, but dozens of times). Impossible to notice changes from one day to the next; impossible not to notice them from one year to the next. Yet many changes were from one day to the next and were severe in their impact. A whole series of 'lasts' obviously occurred: the last day he went to the toilet on his own; the last day he put on his own pants; the last day he used a knife or fork; the last day he was able to scratch his nose; the last day he walked, the last day we ever played 'The bear and the clown' on the lounge room floor…

I doubt if either of my children knew how much I enjoyed seeing them each afternoon, but they knew how much I enjoyed listening to music, and music led to one of our favourite games on the lounge room floor: the bear and the clown.

To set the scene, I need to go back nearly forty years. My classical music education at high school had been simplistic at best: a cross between listening for the cannon in the *1812 Overture*, and imagining the big bad wolf in *Peter and the Wolf*. That all changed one night when I was twenty. Someone bought me a ticket to hear the Sydney Symphony Orchestra conducted by Moshe Atzmon at the Sydney Town Hall. I walked out of that concert a different person.

The SSO played Stravinski's *Petrouchka* that evening. I had never heard a piece of music like it. Every melody and movement created a vivid soundscape in my head. I felt I was listening to the vast expanses of the twentieth century, captured in music before they had actually been traversed. Even though Russian folklore is at the heart of the ballet, the music spoke to me of the rolling prairies of America and the New World as well as the folklore of Europe. Exhilarated, I walked down the street outside the Town Hall that night, boring my companions as I tried to put into words what I had just felt. I was fortunate to know people then who knew far more about art, music and culture than I did, and I lapped up what they had to tell me about the Ballet Russe, Diaghalev, Nijinski, and Stravinski himself. No one would describe *Petrouchka* as avant-garde in 1969, but it transformed what classical music meant to me, taking it out of a box called 'museum culture', and making it part of my daily life.

I was fascinated to learn that Stravinsky had resisted Diaghilev's attempts to get him to change the ending. The fourth and final scene of the score begins with the Shrovetide Fair melody from the first scene, but this time far more melodious, confident, aspirational, in command, dominating. The melody is triumphantly played by the strings, before it is picked up by the horns. At this point, life is still good, the world is still good, the fairground is still a happy place, the stuff of childhood dreams and happiness. All that is best about our natures is played back to us. But these good times do not last. Fear returns, and the music changes, and eventually peters out, not with a bang but a whimper.

There is no hero in this ballet. *Petrouchka*, a clown puppet, is hacked to death by the villain, but returns as a ghost right at the end to haunt his old puppet master. The tensions which result in this anticlimactic yet tragic end are mirrored in the ballet by other tales within a tale, a series of cameo dances, including one – the peasant and the dancing bear – at the point in the story just before the joy of the carnival gives way to the darker passions lying just beneath the surface of puppets and humans alike.

Fast forward twenty-five years to the mid 1990s. For Benjamin and Rosanna's sake, I have taken liberties with the Russian folk tale to suit my own storytelling purposes. It has now become known in the family as 'the bear and the clown', and in the version they have come to love, and love to fear, it is the bear who becomes the villain and who stalks and then destroys the clown. And as I play this final part of *Petrouckha* over and over for them, I act out the part of the bear, stalking them around the lounge room, like some deranged, middle-aged, over the top, maniac, the music as loud as I dare play it in bourgeois Glenelg, and doing my best to frighten the daylights out of both kids, while also showing them how these emotions come through in the music itself. The heavy boom, boom, boom that stalks and finally kills the lyrical melody of the Shrovetide Fair…it is me stomping around the living room like a big, black bear, coming after them.

We would wrestle on the lounge room floor, the scary bear winning every time. The wrestles were particularly delicate balancing acts. On the one hand, I had a boisterous daughter, who did not know the limits of her own strength, and who would play as hard and fast as I would let her (often a little too hard and fast, her teeth embedded in some part of my arm or leg if the going got tough and she got desperate). On the other hand, I had a son who could barely walk, and had little strength. So, at the same time, I was trying to give Rosanna a good tussle while simulating the same thing with Benji. The three of us would be rolling around on the floor, the music blaring.

There were many other styles of music that I introduced my kids to (everything from Philip Glass to Brian Eno to David Bowie to Nusrat Fateh Ali Khan) in this way: after dinner, played loud in the lounge room, an outlandish story I had concocted, and then embellished as time went on, wrestling on the floor mainly because I was too nervous about Benji falling or being knocked over if we were on our feet and dancing. But it is the bear and the clown that sticks in all of our minds as the big one. And it is the bear that gets the final say, not the clown.

Fast forward another fifteen years. The Mawson Chapel at Centennial Park. 5 July 2007. We decide to play a few minutes of the 'bear and the clown' during the service. Benjamin, my *Petrouchka*, hapless and helpless in the face of his own black bear, cut down, yes, but somehow there, above us all, packed into that chapel that cold afternoon.

And probably consulting his *South Australian Almanac* to see when the next king tide was coming, and then the weather reports, hoping the king tide would coincide with a storm.

It is the end of the millennium. 9/11 and all that followed has not yet happened. Ben's angry tirades at the television screen whenever George W. Bush or John Winston Howard appeared had not yet happened. We had lived for a happy decade in Glenelg, but the wheels were turning, and goblins were starting to breach the walls of our house, our shell of refuge. Rosanna was getting closer and closer to puberty. The simple fairy tale of mummy, daddy, little boy and little girl, living together like this happily ever after, would not go on forever, or even much longer. Development was also underway in the sleepy holiday suburb of Glenelg. New apartment blocks and shops were going up; suddenly, the suburb had become a hot real estate market. Landmarks that seemed fixed and unchanging were changing. Old houses on both sides of our street were being demolished and built over. The old kiosk near where we lived was slated for demolition.

Meanwhile, an orthopaedic surgeon had been measuring the gradual bending of the bones in Ben's spine, and by the start of 2000, the angle had got to more than 30%, and a decision point had been reached: to have the operation which fuses two steel rods from the collar bone to the pelvis, thereby holding up the whole body mechanically, just like a skyscraper, and leaving the lungs as much room as possible to do their job. The operation lasts four or five hours, and the decision was made to have it in February 2000. Why February? To give Ben as much of that summer at the beach as possible, as well as enough time to recover before the dangers of colder weather arrived. The coming operation dominated my thoughts for the months leading up to it, and made me look at the spectacular millennial fireworks that New Year's Eve in Sydney with more than usual foreboding and dread.

Everything was becoming more serious, more threatening, more interconnected. Even the necessary anaesthetics posed an above average risk to Benjamin's chances of surviving the procedure. A couple of my churchgoing colleagues organised a mass for Benjamin on the morning of the operation. I dropped my mother off at St Francis Xavier's Cathedral in the city on the way to the hospital to sit out the operation in North Adelaide. I got there just in time to see Benji being wheeled into the operating theatre. He looked vulnerable and defenceless, but also stoic and calm.

It was a forty-degree day. Esther and I walked aimlessly around the hot streets of North Adelaide, able to do nothing except wait for the time to head back to the hospital. The operation was a success, even though the convalescence was slow and painful. Like other boys who have spinal fusion surgery, Benji was a couple of centimetres taller after the operation than he was before. He had also lost all flexibility in his back. From now on, he would bend at the hips, never at the waist. He was part cyborg.

We were sufficiently concerned that he would not make it through the operation that we decided to get a pet dog for Rosanna before the surgery. I guess most teenage girls get a white fluffy pet puppy because they want one; Rosanna got one just in case her brother died on the operating table. But that is how the funny little dog called Cristal, with one blue eye and one black eye, came into our lives, as a kind of insurance policy for Rosanna.

The irony is that Cristal became a very important part of the rest of Benji's life. He loved that dog. She would jump up onto his lap as soon as he got home from school and then, later, TAFE. She somehow sensed that Benji couldn't get into the house himself, that someone had to open the front door for him. Every afternoon, when it came about time for Ben's access cab to pull up out the front, Cristal would start to become restless. As soon as she heard the taxi outside, she would become even more agitated, and come to one of us, barking, jumping against our legs, demanding immediate action. She only calmed down when we moved to open the door to let Benji in, even if, at that point, the driver was still only at the point of unbuckling the wheelchair in the van.

On the last afternoon of Benji's life, Cristal spent about an hour on Ben's lap, his chair tilted back to give her a more stable sitting space. They both soaked up the winter sun in my backyard. She would get up by jumping onto a low outdoor sofa Ben had parked next to, and then jump across to him. As often was the case, he would talk to her, and she would yap back – something she only did for him.

Cristal is the kind of little terrier that barks aggressively when a stranger comes to the door. Many 'strangers' came to my door in the few days after Ben died, but she didn't bark once. She just lay down in a corner of the room, and kept to herself. A week or so later, after the funeral, she resumed her barking routine when anyone came to the house. My mother pointed this little detail out to me. And Cristal was there to give Rosanna comfort when she did lose her brother, seven years later than in the original scenario. The insurance policy had been honoured.

I didn't see it clearly at the time, but the arrival of Cristal into our house was a turning point. The fairy tale in Glenelg was coming to an end, just as a century was coming to an end. Everything was changing. Benjamin's disease was demanding serious and sustained attention. Its demands on all of us could no longer be denied. I knew I was starting to struggle with the unceasing build-up of stress and frustration and dread. Cristal was a warm and affectionate companion for Ben and for us, a diversion from fear and melancholy. And she still is a warm and loveable link to Ben for his sister and mother and me. But Cristal's arrival in our lives was not innocent. A new and darker day had dawned. Cristal came with the new millennium, with a new Glenelg, and a new phase in all our lives. She is now well into doggy middle-age. When Cristal goes, we will lose a part of Ben all over again.

4

100 Millilitres of Water, 24 Grams of Life

A hundred millilitres of water. Yesterday, I used a forty-millimetre medicine cup to put this much into a glass, and then I drank it in one gulp. It's not very much. There were days, not so long ago, when the whole purpose and meaning of existence revolved around mouthfuls of water just like this.

Every brain cell in my head would be focused on getting Ben to drink this much liquid. It was not possible to concentrate on anything else. If and when he did, I was elated, it was better than any victory, a small step had been taken on the road back to recovery, to normalcy, to home, to life outside the hospital ward. If he didn't, I would try and hide my dread, try and stay positive, try and put the best possible light on it. We would improvise, adding cordial from the ward fridge to make it more appetising; we would use orange juice; we would try and do anything to get some liquids into him. The nurses made it very obvious without exactly saying so that his survival, not just gradual recovery, depended on fluids, especially when he had a fever. When the fever was at its worst, he would be getting liquids through an intravenous drip, but those intensive periods were different to what I am describing here. Those were crisis periods, where everything was in doubt, including his life. I am talking here about the next phase: the long days, and the long succession of days, when he would be slowly, slowly, improving, and the odds were more likely that he would be coming home again, to fight another day.

The days I am talking about: he is a little better, but not well;

conscious, but not himself; able to interact, but not wanting to. He has been exhausted by his pneumonia, and is only recovering in the tiniest of increments, one mouthful of water at a time.

How many days were there like this? Many days. Hospital. Once upon a time, the word hardly registered in my consciousness. The word fills me with feelings of horror and dread now. Like other boys with Duchenne muscular dystrophy, from the time Ben was twelve or so, our dealings with the hospital system began to increase and multiply.

In retrospect, I can see that these hospital experiences fell into four main categories. On the bottom rung were reconnaissance visits to specialists (respiratory physicians, cardiologists, orthopaedic surgeons and so on) as part of the ongoing monitoring of the 'progress' of Ben's disease. On the next rung were medicalised versions of overnight stays in motels: overnights spent in sleep units with Ben hooked up to all sorts of machines and monitors, the purpose being to chart the quality of his sleep, and the decline in how well he was able to inhale oxygen and exhale carbon dioxide when he was asleep and his lungs were at their most relaxed, and therefore least effective. One step further up the ladder was admission to hospital for a planned procedure, such as the muscle biopsy when he was a baby, or the spinal fusion operation when he was fifteen. And then, by far the worst on this scale of dread, there was the final rung: admission because he had become too sick (with pneumonia, or the flu, or a chest infection) to be cared for at home, and his life was at risk.

Ben had four such 'level four' periods in hospital, and each of them lasted for about two weeks. Three of the four were very serious, were life-threatening. He could easily have died, twice, in 2006. I believe he would have died on one of those occasions if Esther had not been there with him during the night, as she was every night, and kept his throat clear enough to keep him breathing.

Being with him, and not knowing if he would pull through, and being with him but not enjoying the normal pleasures of his company, because he was too sick to laugh or talk, were morale-sapping ordeals for me, as they must have been for Esther too. The first time he had pneumonia, in July 2002, I was so frightened by what it meant now for him to get a cold or a runny nose, that for the next two winters, I crossed off the the days in my diary between Anzac Day (the unofficial start of the rainy season in Adelaide) and the opening of the Adelaide Show and the coming of spring. A hundred and thirty-five days, if the show started on 5 September. For those two winters, I crossed the days off one by one, noting little milestones like getting halfway through winter without incident, until we got to that turning point in the calendar when we could all start looking forward to warmer weather again, to the end of the flu season, to summer. He made it through 2003 and 2004 unscathed, had one less serious stay in 2005, two near fatal stays in 2006, and had not reached the halfway mark of the 2007 cold season before we lost him at the end of June – to heart, not lung, failure.

On each of these four occasions, we knew the hospital did not have enough staff to properly attend to his needs. For one thing, he had no way of getting the nurses' attention if he needed them. So we divided each twenty-four-hour period up into two shifts. Esther took the night shifts and I took the day shifts. Both had their pros and cons. Nearly every minute of his total time in hospital was like this, with a little bit of help a couple of times a week from other family members or friends. Words do not easily describe how demanding those twelve-hour periods stretching for twelve to fourteen consecutive days were.

There were many serious things to notice and think about: temperature during fever, oxygen saturations levels, discharge of spit and mucus and other bad stuff from the lungs and throat, eating and drinking, urinating. Chest physio, suction tubes, oximeters, cough machines, paper tissues, little cups of cordial or juice – these things became our whole world.

Peter Rose puts it well in his account of his brother's early days in hospital after a car accident that left him permanently paralysed:

> Robert's bed, his condition, its fluctuations, were the focus of our devastated universe. Watching him, charting his progress, noting

each flicker of improvement, it was possible to forget other certainties and to believe, however innocently, in some sort of rehabilitated meaning. His illness was our cause, our cosmology. We were beginning to orbit him, needful and responsive, just like him. (Rose, pp. 110–111)

These periods in hospital were long enough to get to know some of the rituals from the inside, but not so long that the oddities of the situation had become so pervasive as to become invisible. The way the doctors fell into rank according to their status in the pecking order was almost comical at times. The way they walked around the wards said all you needed to know about who was in charge and who wasn't.

And below the doctors stretched a long line of lower forms of life in the hospital hierarchy: nurses, nursing aides, physiotherapists, social workers, caterers, cleaners, TV men, the occasional chaplain or volunteer, other people in the ward and their regular visitors. And all of this became our whole world at the same as Ben's life was in the balance. It was too intense at the time to think about, but now I can see why illnesses such as pneumonia are seen so often in dramaturgical terms. It is the ultimate drama. Fighting pneumonia, when your defences are weak and already seriously breached, is a titanic struggle which could go either way.

We learnt to calibrate our anxiety and attention levels more according to what the more experienced nurses did or did not say, rather than on what the doctors said. During his first bout with pneumonia, I ran into one of his specialists in the cafeteria. In two unguarded minutes, I learnt more from him than I had in the previous week when he had been doing his rounds in the ward. I learnt that he genuinely thought the outcome was uncertain, that in his view Ben's fate was no longer going to be decided by what sophisticated treatments he or a modern hospital could provide. (Looking back, I suppose Doctor X believed both things – the calm, judicious nod when he saw us 'officially' in the ward, and the sense of doubt and even helplessness that he revealed to me in the cafeteria. But now I also know that even then the system in South Australia was not providing all the resources that could have been provided, and are provided in other places, and the doctor must have known this also, and had to live and work with this knowledge. But this book is about Ben, and the resources and systems he had to live with, not those provided in other possible worlds.)

These two-week stays in hospital (a time when everything else in my life stopped, had to stop) each divided into three parts: the first was the initial crisis, when there was high fever, lungs filling with liquid, no sign of improvement, and the outcome very much in doubt; the second was when the fever appeared to break and some clearing up seemed to be going on in the lungs, and there was real hope that he might get better; and the third was the recovery, as Ben very slowly and gradually returned to enough of his normal self to be able to go home. Less significant versions of this cycle also occurred regularly, with each day having its own crises, setbacks, small victories, and false dawns.

And so it was that a hundred millilitres of water became the ultimate precious commodity. Whole days became focused on just one thing: fluids in, fluids out. Some nurses clearly relied more on the colour and quantity of Ben's urine than any other single measure of whether he was getting better or not. The more the better, the less orange and the clearer, the better. We would have pages to fill in, tabulating how much he drank, when; how much he urinated, when. And I also used to keep my own tallies, just for something to do, setting both of us little goals: one hundred millilitres before lunch, two hundred millilitres before dinner. It is hard to believe now, but in that situation, every aspect of my life came down to this one burning obsession: to reach the goals we needed to reach in terms of drinking enough fluids to know he is getting better. There were numerous times when he wouldn't, or couldn't, drink at all. I am not surprised. It must be hard to drink when you feel you are drowning in your own body's secretions. At such times, he would be hooked up to an intravenous drip.

By the end of his second stay in August 2006, I knew that I was close to breaking point. I knew I didn't have the strength to keep this level of intense routine up any more if he was admitted again. I arranged with various friends and family members to be able to come for a few hours a week, to provide some respite for us. We also asked the doctor to have Ben classified as a high(er)-needs patient, which meant he would have been put in a ward with higher than normal numbers of nursing staff.

Of course, the system could never admit that it was unable to fully attend to Ben's needs, so we, his parents, were there as if we were 'just' visitors, even though we did most of the work of looking after him, because we felt we had very little choice if we wanted to do the best for our son. We also tried to use up some of our carer hours provided by the government, but the hospital would not permit our carers to do any caring for Ben, like feeding him or washing him, because it would have raised complex duty of care issues if anything had gone wrong. Of course, the health system could not and would not be forced into acknowledging its own limitations in such a public way.

Most of the time, regardless of the stage he was at in the pneumonia cycle, Ben could do absolutely nothing for himself. He couldn't get himself a drink, even if he had wanted one. He couldn't remove the phlegm from his mouth. He couldn't use the buzzer to call for attention. He relied totally on someone noticing him, and inferring what his needs might be. It slowly dawned on me that hospitals are designed for 'normal' people who get sick or have an accident; they are not designed for disabled people who get sick. In fact, they are as clumsy in their ability to respond in a fine-tuned way to the needs of people with serious disabilities as most other public institutions, like cathedrals, universities, art galleries and the rest.

Even though Ben would always manage a smile for a visitor, it must have been dreadful for him most of the time. We wiped saliva, phlegm and chest infection secretions from his mouth and lips hundreds, if not thousands, of times in a typical day. Who would have done that for him if we had not been there? What would have happened if it had not been done? What would it be like to be in Ben's position as your throat fills up with mucus, and you cannot get the attention of anyone to clear it for you? They say the Eskimos have dozens of words for snow. I don't have the vocabulary to describe the different types of mucus-type secretions that came out of Ben's mouth: variations in colour, quantity, viscosity, frothiness, and on it goes.

One day, I calculated the number of times I got up from the chair next to his bed to do something for him. Five minutes might pass and there was nothing to do; but then there might be five minutes when he needed his throat cleared of brown stuff coming up from his lungs every few seconds. I averaged it out at about five such 'interventions' a minute, or three hundred an hour, or 3,600 in a twelve-hour shift, or over 40,000 in a two-week stay. Surely it couldn't have been as intense as that? Yet it was. The only way for me to keep on keeping on was to concentrate on the very short term – the next ten minutes – and think as little as possible about the bigger picture: how many more weeks would or could this go on for? Would it end in taking him home again?

Ben, how did you feel? At times I know you were frightened, but just how frightened I will never know. How did you feel when all the usual places on your body for taking blood samples had become pockmarked with unsuccessful attempts, and it became unbearable for me to look at the purple bruises on your forearms? You never showed the slightest fear of the pain of getting a needle or having some object inserted into you. I don't know how you did that, son, I really don't. How did you feel when you were full of mucus you were unable to cough up, and you must have felt like you were drowning in your own liquids, totally reliant on others to stand there and wipe the stuff away with a paper tissue or with the suction tube?

Thank goodness for the suction tube! How much easier it was to clear your mouth of stuff, often amounting in quantity to little more than a viscous pea. Watching the container behind the bed gradually fill up with the secretions from your chest, making sure the tip of the suction tube didn't get dirty, changing it regularly, emptying the container, washing the tube with distilled water. The suction sounds. The knowledge that every bit of phlegm out was a step that was not in the wrong direction even if it meant little as a sign of progress in itself.

Esther and I would change shifts around nine o'clock at night, when we would sometimes work together to toilet or shower Ben. It goes without saying that we had no time to sit down together over a coffee and talk about the situation at hand, or talk about Ben, or talk about how we were coping, or talk about anything at all. She needed me to remain in working order; I needed her to stay the same way. Ben needed us both. By the time Esther arrived, I was usually exhausted, hungry and highly stressed, and would have to restrain myself from running out of the hospital. By the time I arrived back the next morning, she was feeling much the same way.

It takes me about twenty minutes to read the daily newspaper when I am in my normal routine. On those days in the ward, the newspapers piled up. I hardly ever finished a full newspaper in any twenty-four-hour period. The days became defined by humdrum markers of time passing, such as the theme songs of the various repeat TV programs playing on the various sets that patients in the ward had hired. Replays of *Mash* were a particular marker for me. The show would come on at 5 p.m. I would hear the familiar tune, one of my favourites, and I would know that the main systems of the hospital were rapidly winding down for the night, and just as importantly, that I was on the final stretch of my 'shift' before being replaced by Esther. In the 1970s, if someone had said that I would be measuring out my life to the tune of *Mash* and thimbles of water, my powers of extrapolation would have failed me.

How did I survive these aspects of Ben's life? I know I came close to breaking down on more than one occasion. (There is reasonable evidence now that I did have some kind of breakdown, but that is another story.) Those hospital stays were made harder because the weeks and days leading up to admission were filled with anxiety, as Ben appeared to be coming down with some kind of cold or sore throat. He had a personality which would deny anything was wrong until he really couldn't avoid it any more. (Who could blame him in those circumstances? We were in the hospital half the time; he was there 24/7, and he was the one in high fever, fighting for breath and drowning in the liquids filling up his lungs.) On the other hand, I have a personality which sees the worst case scenario too easily, and I would be thinking he should be at the hospital being checked out while Ben would be maintaining a stoic attitude that he was really OK. These disagreements were very stressful. No one was in the wrong, and no one was in the right. The closest we all came to misjudging the situation was in July 2006, when his lungs stopped completely while he was in the casualty waiting area with his mother.

We survived in our different ways, and as best we could. It would be difficult for me to ever judge another human being in this situation harshly, no matter what careless acts they might do or how selfish their reactions might be. In my case, I think I also managed to get by in one of the ways Viktor Frankl writes that he survived Auschwitz – through curiosity:

> Cold curiosity predominated even in Auschwitz, somehow detaching the mind from its surroundings, which came to be regarded with a kind of objectivity. At that time one cultivated this state of mind as a means of protection. We were anxious to know what would happen next; and what would be the consequence, for example, of our standing in the open air, in the chill of late autumn, stark naked, and still wet from the showers. In the next few days our curiosity evolved into surprise; surprise that we did not catch cold. (Frankl, pp. 14–15)

Even though curiosity failed me during Ben's most intense struggles with pneumonia, it was also something I often felt in the face of the inexorable progress of his disease: curiosity, and with it a certain kind of practical problem-solving instinct or response. Such and such is now the case…how does this change what we did before? What new alternatives do we have? How have the odds changed? And so on.

There were indeed several occasions when the advanced nature of medical technology was interesting for its own sake. I vividly remember the journey up Ben's penis, through the grey blob that the technician described as his prostate gland, and into his relatively capacious bladder. I watched the whole journey on a television screen, holding his hand. It reminded me of caving, of going into a spherical, limestone cave. As the tiny torch is shone on different parts of the roof and walls of the cave, I can see a grey, fairly smooth, surface. Coming from this wet rock, I could see what looked like little 'puffs' or bursts of a fine mist or spray. The doctor controlling the torch marvelled at what he thought was the fine state of Ben's bladder, and informed us that this fine mist we could see on the screen was urine being emitted by the kidneys into the bladder. In such situations, yes, a cold curiosity was a plus, and helped me survive this invasion of my son's body.

I suppose the number of times Ben was in hospital with pneumonia was about average for someone with his disease. I have known others who have spent more times in hospital, and some who have spent less. Whatever the case, when the long-awaited day would arrive for his discharge, I would wake up feeling like I was a kid again, and it was my birthday. The day felt irresistibly hopeful and special.

Leaving the ward was a massive undertaking. Ben would insist on saying goodbye individually to every other patient in the ward, and that would take precious time. As we moved to the exits with all his stuff, it must have looked like we were rich but eccentric people checking out of a grand hotel, loaded down with our unconventional luggage.

On the last time we went through this transition, in August 2006, we were headed down South Road on the way home. Ben was excited, commenting on all the little details you see as you drive along, ordinary things you notice with new relish if you have been in a hospital bed for the last fortnight. We decided to stop at the twenty-four-hour Vili's café, located in the grounds of their pie and pastry factory. I pulled into the car park, got the ramp out, got Ben out of the van, and then we made our way into the busy café. It was approaching noon, and the shop was full of customers, most of them wearing their Vili's uniforms. (The oddity of these people, spending their mornings making these things, and then their lunch hours eating them, amused both of us.) We were both feeling hungry by now, and really looking forward to a pie or a sausage roll. Ben's happiness at being out of hospital at last also added to the celebratory atmosphere.

The café was not easy to negotiate in a wheelchair. Once inside, Ben realised that he needed to go to the toilet, and that it couldn't wait till after we had something to eat and drove home. The thing was – once the thought had formed in his mind that he had to urinate, he could think of nothing else until he had done so. The sausage roll would have to wait until we had found a disabled toilet, and completed the laborious process of relieving this bodily need.

We followed the familiar wheelchair icon, down a narrow, cluttered corridor. The toilet was there, all right, but the entrance was completely blocked by cartons of fruit juices and soft drinks. Using it was out of the question. Unnecessary delays were also out of the question.

The celebratory stop at Vili's had turned into an unpleasant, stressful ordeal, as we went through the whole thing in reverse, getting back into the van, to get home as quickly as possible. For a few moments, I felt both anger and defeat. Why is it so hard for Ben to even have the pleasure of a sausage roll? He's just been in hospital for two weeks. Why this, why now?

Back in the van, back on South Road again, our eyes made contact in the rear-vision mirror. We were hovering on the edge – somewhere between fury and despair. But in a flash, the anger and stress drained out of both our faces. We grinned, and then laughed, a hollow laugh maybe, but still a laugh. 'Those bastards can take their sausage rolls and stick them you know where,' he yelled. And so we spent the rest of the trip outdoing each other in rhetorical excess. I will never be able to think about a Vili's sausage roll the same way again.

5

It Can't Be Helped

I am lying stretched out on my side, in the narrow space between Ben's shower/toilet chair and the side wall of my small toilet. There was a time when we had an easier set-up for such toileting and showering, after we had spent $20,000 building a new accessible bathroom for Ben's use in our Californian bungalow in beachside Glenelg. But that time has passed, and I am now living in a more modest house, one which my children had helped me find, about a block from an inner-city railway station, and I didn't have a spare few thousand dollars any longer to spend on a new disability-friendly toilet, and even if I did, the space couldn't be made any bigger anyway without some serious demolition.

And this is why I am now lying on my side, in a cramped, uncomfortable position, looking up at dark shadows above me which I know to be Ben's thighs and nether regions.

1. Twist and pull the seal of nozzle. 2. Squeeze the tube slightly so that a drop of microlax smears the tip and makes insertion easier. 3. Insert the nozzle fully into the rectum (children under three only insert nozzle halfway). 4. Squeeze out the contents fully by squeezing the shoulder of the tube. 5. Keeping the tube squeezed tightly, withdraw the nozzle.

On one level, I suppose this is quite a normal, if generally solitary, thing to do. Most people, if they are doing it to themselves, are probably doing it by touch and feel rather than by sight. (Use of the verb 'to do' here strikes me as a little odd, though apt; it feels like when 'do' is used in place of 'having sex'.) Ben is a young man, and I am trying to get this thing in, and help him 'go' – the sooner the better, the more the better – so we can progress to the next stage of getting to bed. I am afraid of hurting him, because at some point I just have to go for it, based on what he tells me he can feel, and I hope I have found my target.

I don't think we hit too many wrong targets over the years. But we did have one major crisis, when he wasn't able to go for well over a week. Constipation leads to complications. Constipation leads to hospitalisation. It's not good. As the days pass without success, the anxiety and tension increase. Each attempt at going to the toilet becomes more anticipated yet more dreaded. It was not uncommon for Ben to spend well over an hour on the toilet chair, at considerable internal and external physical discomfort to himself. He never complained about it, but it must have been difficult, wanting to go but not being able to, feeling this unmoving, unwanted load resting heavily in your gut, knowing someone else is sweating on you to finish, and not letting their anxiety get to you. Sometimes, he would need his legs lifted off the by-now hard surface of the chair, to relieve the pressure for a few seconds. His legs were a heavy, dead weight, like the rest of him. It wasn't easy giving him this temporary relief.

It is a grim situation to find yourself in. Living well has come down to this: success or not on the toilet. But this statement is as true as it is misleading. This poking around in the dark that I described above would most of the time take place while my opinionated young man would be arguing with me about politics, or making a joke about something, or just musing to us both about some aspect of life that he had noticed and been intrigued by, his thoughts off in some strange planetary orbit, way outside ground control.

The point is this. If we think of conventional levels of dignity and personal privacy as akin to the seven veils of Salome, then Ben had no choice but to be stripped of all seven veils by this stage in his dance through life. He had become naked, unaccommodated man, most of the usual props, props that protect our dignity by means of an obsessive adherence to personal privacy, thrown away, beside the point. And yet. And yet his dignity was untouched by any of this, and didn't need any of the usual props to maintain a genuine level of appropriate self-respect. I wonder if most of us get through most of our lives without having any certain idea whether we have been able to keep our dignity and self-respect intact or not? We don't know because we are never quite free of the usual props that protect us from the full consequences of the alternatives. Maybe we didn't have much real dignity to begin with.

Benjamin had the temperament to accept situations he couldn't change, and to just get on with living, adapting to his new terms of reference. This would be an achievement under most circumstances, but to be able to maintain this outlook on life while dealing with dozens and dozens of these morale-sapping changes… This is why I have to tell his story as best I can.

It is this aspect of muscular dystrophy that is the real challenge, as far as I can see. On the one hand, you are born with this terrible affliction, one which, by the end of your short life, will be so overwhelming that people like me will wonder how you can be so unable to help yourself and yet still be able to live. On the other hand, you only get the full affliction in tiny, gradual doses. When the end comes, it is the logical culmination of dozens of small defeats, stretching over decades, for those organs and cells in the body responsible for its security and defence.

Were there any losses or setbacks that had any positive, albeit unintended, consequences? I can only think of two. When Ben had become too weak to be pushed around in a manual chair, and was assigned his first electric wheelchair, that was a plus. He could drive where he wanted to go, stop when he wanted to, and go at his own pace. It also meant that we didn't have to push him everywhere. And the second plus? It is a terrible thing to say, but I had the benefit of far more of his company than I otherwise would have had if he had not been so dependent on me. I got to know and enjoy Ben as a young adult far more than my father ever knew or enjoyed me. By the end, Ben had become my closest friend, my mate. We spent a lot of time together from the time he finished high school. He was my friend in the sense that what I might be musing to myself and what I could say to him had become very close to the same thing. For example, I might be driving along, and see something that I thought was odd or noteworthy. What I would be thinking to myself and what I would likely say to Ben if he was in the van with me were one and the same thing, in tone, language and content.

But I digress. From birth, inside his body, the forces of weakness were battling the forces of strength, and every single one of those battles ended in defeat. Big defeats, like no longer being able to get himself up off the floor, or stand, or walk, or get dressed, or feed himself, or roll over in bed, or wipe his own bottom. And small defeats, like no longer having the strength to eat something he loved, like a fresh apple, or scratch an itchy nose, or brush away a fly or a mosquito. There must have been a specific day in Ben's life when each of these things, and thousands of others, happened for the last time. And each time, he had to adapt, to keep on going, to look forward to what he could do, and not dwell on what he couldn't.

Yes, muscular dystrophy is a strange and challenging adversary. When Ben began at Mitcham Primary School, he was part of a special group of kids from Regency Park (then known as the Crippled Children's Association) who were being 'mainstreamed' at Mitcham in a new integration program in a 'normal' suburban school. I often collected Benji after school in those years (1991–1994), because the special bus trip home used to take over an hour and make his days very long. I would be in the school car park when the kids would come running and screaming out of their classrooms; eventually, Benji would appear, walking slowly, as best he could. At that time, he didn't look disabled at all. Every other kid in that special program looked more disabled than he did. But as the years went by, Ben caught up with them, and passed them all, one by one. Several of them were at his funeral, still looking much the same as they did all those years ago. Jane, Aaron, Alison, Todd, Michael…your names and faces are coming back to me. He was lucky to be part of that pioneering group of kids with 'special needs', as well as their teachers, carers and families, in primary school. We were lucky. Not quite so lucky in high school, where friends were harder to find, the schoolwork more demanding, his physical needs greater, and where another boy in a wheelchair often picked on him. One disabled boy being bullied by another disabled boy. Not so hard to believe, when you think about it. I saw that young man making his way on his own through the city a few months after Ben had died. He still looked angry, still unhappy. He was still in his wheelchair.

I do not know how Ben kept his spirits up as much as he did through such a long, inexorable process of gradual decline. But the fact is that he did. There were not many times when it seemed to become too much for him. But it took its toll on him and his spirit, I have no doubt about that.

When Rosanna went to New Zealand with her boyfriend Tim in late 2006, she put her travel diary on the web – pictures and accounts of her adventures. Ben never went to that site to have a look for himself at what his sister was up to. When I asked him about it, he told me it made him too sad; it was something he so craved to be able to do himself, but of course it was out of the question. He felt no resentment that Rosanna was doing these things with her life. But he couldn't bear facing the fact that he couldn't do these outdoor things himself.

I will spend longer describing the other incident. It was one of the very few times in his life when I think he felt…defeated. Beyond angry; anger had lost its point. Beaten into submission by forces internal and external that he could no longer control or even much influence.

It was about a fortnight before his death, and I had driven to the Julia Farr Centre to pick him up for the day, which would be spent with me at my house. I would time my arrival to occur just after he had had lunch and was dressed and ready to roll. More often than not, he would be waiting for me downstairs when I got there. (My son so looking forward to seeing me? I was a lucky dad, I really was.) But this time, he was still on his bed – an anomalous detail with the benefit of hindsight, but which didn't occur to me as such in the heat of the moment.

'Some things in this world can't be helped,' he said. 'And I believe this is probably one of them.' Cormac McCarthy, you could have been writing those words for what had happened to my son that day.

Benjamin didn't say much on this particular day, he didn't say much at all. And he wasn't still in bed. My mind has tricked me. That false detail I've just mentioned comes to my mind first, because it was when he was back on his bed that he gave me the look, the expression, that I am writing about here. Of course he wasn't in bed. It was two o'clock in the afternoon, and he was in his chair. But what he was, was wet, really, really wet. One of the biggest wees I can recall having to clean up, and one of the freshest, if that is the right word. Still warm. It must have happened just as I arrived. While I was in the lift to his floor. I now ask myself, for the first time since that incident, whether he had asked for assistance. But what's the point? The staff were probably too busy or too preoccupied to notice anything out of the ordinary. This was the Huntington's ward, after all. I will never know now, and it doesn't really matter. No system on earth can cope with someone with Ben's needs every single time, without fail.

My first reaction was anger. Ben, you are twenty-two years old, how could this happen? You know your own body. There are staff here who are paid to look after you. That is their job. Why does the first hour we have together today have to be spent like this? There are so many things we would both prefer to be doing. And then there was my frustration. And the thrashing around for relief from the frustration. Blame is always a good outlet, comforting and fortifying myself with the knowledge that it is someone else's fault.

'It's all for the best.' This is another way of making sense of these lousy twists and turns of fate. This was my mother's philosophy, and I have these words flowing in my veins – the constant (neurotic?) need to find some silver lining in the darkest of clouds. Optimist or fool? Endless scenarios, like 'It's all for the best that we didn't go out today, because there's been a big storm.' Or is it a form of nihilism? The redeeming clause following the statement of a negative, as in 'Just as well we didn't have more food, otherwise we might have all got fat and died of a heart attack.' Or a form of *felix culpa*? Life is bad, yes, but there must be bad in order for there to be such a thing as good. Without sin, no redemption; without Adam and Eve, no need for Jesus Christ. The idea is as old as religion.

In this instance, I struggle to believe it. There are some things which do not have enough redeeming features, and Benjamin's disease was one of them. And Benjamin knew it that day, sitting in his own hot piss, defeated. I can just about comprehend that Jesus Christ might have sacrificed himself for the rest of us, but at least he had a choice. Benjamin had no such choice.

In the months after Ben's death, a concerned friend recommended that I read Victor Frankl's well-known book, *From Death Camp to Existentialism*. It was a good choice. Frankl's insights had been earned inside Nazi concentration camps. I can trust him. Frankl had looked Benjamin's predicament – the lack of any active choice – in the face, and still found some meaning:

> An active life serves the purpose of giving man the opportunity to realise values in creative work, while a passive life of enjoyment affords him the opportunity to obtain fulfilment in experiencing beauty, art, or nature. But there is a purpose in life which is almost barren of both creation and enjoyment and which admits of but one possibility of high moral behaviour: namely, in man's attitude to his existence, an existence restricted by external forces. A creative life and a life of enjoyment are banned to him. But not only creativeness and enjoyment are meaningful. If there is a meaning in life at all, then there must be a meaning in suffering. Suffering is an ineradicable part of life, even as fate and death. Without suffering and death human life cannot be complete. (Frankl, p. 67)

He captures the tension in Ben's adult life well: a life being lived for the most part beyond the possibility of either creative work or active enjoyments. He seems to be saying that, no matter how grim what happens to you may be, there is still the opportunity to adopt an attitude towards what is happening to you, and that attitude will be what gives you some ineradicable dignity and meaning in life.

If that is so, then the urination incident I am describing here comes very close to being Ben's own dark night of the soul, when he nearly gave up hope.

Normally, when I was confronted with a very stressful situation, like this one, he would meet my anger with his own anger, or with a blithe indifference, or with humour, or an attempt to calm me down. But this day, he said nothing; on his face was the look of someone who had just been served up one wearying challenge or problem too many; he didn't have the resilience, at that moment, to know what attitude to adopt to his predicament.

Within minutes, I had calmed down and was occupied with the task at hand, of getting him out of the chair, onto the bed, clothes off, cleaned up, clothes on, and back into the chair. Nearly an hour later, we were ready to get into the van and head out. We had both bounced back, and were talking as we usually did. The Julia Farr Centre was not far from his old primary school. Absorbed in our chit-chat, I took a wrong turn, and was headed into the street where the school was.

'Dad, turn around, turn around now. Go back.'

Nearly a decade earlier, on his last day at Mitcham Primary School, Ben had vowed never to set foot inside his old school again. As far as I knew, his primary school days were mostly happy. I wonder what had happened, or what fixation had formed in his mind, to make him still so adamant on this point nearly a decade later? I only had to think of how this bladder incident affected me to realise that some events in life are so painful, or attract such unnoticed reservoirs of pain to them, that they become avoided at all costs.

That afternoon, I found some relief by finding someone to blame.

What had happened was this. I had been responsible for buying extra supplies of the latex sheaths that are put over the penis. The sheaths are then attached to a tube which flows inside the trouser leg into a bag held in place around the leg calf by velcro straps. It is a brilliant invention. Toileting can be deferred (especially handy when out in public or if he is on his own) and the process is much simpler and less time-consuming – just emptying the bag. The sheaths are held securely in place on the penis by some kind of adhesive substance, a substance that is not that easy to remove, and for which special remover wipes exist. (What I am describing here must be second nature to thousands of males with continence issues, and a foreign country to nearly everyone else.) Yes, hairs also got stuck, and yes, it was very painful for him when it came time to 'unglue' the sheath from the penis.

For years, Ben had only felt comfortable having these things fitted on, or taken off, by his parents. (It did mean manhandling a young man's penis, after all.) But once he had accepted being cared for at the Julia Farr Centre, he changed his attitude on such matters, and allowed the staff to do it for him. And so it was that on most afternoons when I went to pick him up, or when a taxi was called for him, he was already 'tubed up', as we used to put it.

Unfortunately, this latest batch of rubber sheaths was well past their use-by date when they were shipped from the Adelaide supplier, and the adhesive substance had long since perished. There was nothing holding this flimsy bit of latex in place. So, when Ben had had his lunch, and plenty to drink, he must have decided to urinate, confident that the tube and everything was in working order, and not preoccupied with the constant worry about urinating that dominated many of his waking moments for many years. So the urine would have gone everywhere, and it did. As I was the one cleaning him up, I was the one to discover that the sheaths were out of date and useless. I was the one filled with anger and rage.

As usual with many things to do with being disabled, the arm of government which funds the necessary provision of resources, the arm of government which determines if these resources are necessary in the first place, and the arm of government (or more commonly now, an outsourced provider) which delivers the resource needed (in this case, sheaths, bags, removal wipes, and so on) are separate entities. It's good in theory, and even sometimes in practice. Of course, by giving the client greater responsibility for managing their own affairs, authorities can more easily escape their own, especially when the client must deal with more than one agency for even very simple needs.

And so it was later that afternoon that I found myself on the telephone abusing someone in a warehouse in Melbourne. The poor staff member who took my call barely knew where Adelaide was, but that warehouse was a link in the chain that led to Ben being supplied with defective sheaths. It was bad enough that it happened when and how it did. But it could have happened in a restaurant or shopping mall, or a long way from the supplies and equipment needed to dry and clean him up. It could have been a shameful public humiliation. Ben relied on those sheaths for much of his independence in his last few years. That they could fail him, that he couldn't count on them when he needed to, must have been a tough blow for him. I am not surprised that for a few minutes he had lost his will to fight, the resilience and the will to carry on, even the will to get angry, whether at the system, at the world, or at me.

Anger. I wonder if much thought is ever given to the bouts of anger that seem to me now to be inevitable in any carer-dependent relationship, especially if there is a blood relationship between the two parties. Anger between adolescents and their parents is common enough, so it must be all the more intense when these extra stresses are superimposed on the regular struggles between the generations. There were times when dealing with Ben would make me so angry that I could barely see straight, let alone concentrate on what I was doing. I would be doing my very best to get through what had to be done, and he would be abusing me for my 'incompetence', the word he would use, no doubt because it was so unfair and so certain to goad me. I knew I was slower than his other carers or his mother, and my routines must have been slightly different, but I was doing my best, under trying circumstances, and I could not see why he would not acknowledge that, and at least give me credit for trying. Getting him into bed was a process that lasted about two hours from turning off the TV to turning off the bedroom light, and sometimes it was very unpleasant. Sometimes, I would be so stressed that I would leave him, halfway into the sling used for getting him out of his chair, or half undressed, and go out into the backyard for a minute or two, dry retching. Sometimes I would be in tears – tears, not of sorrow, but of sheer frustration.

We both knew that we should try and manage our anger better. When my mother visited in September 2006, it was obvious to her that I could not continue without some help, and that I was going downhill myself. My routine was to be with Ben from late Friday afternoon to Sunday night after dinner. I would go to work on Monday mornings so tired that it already felt like Friday afternoon. Keeping on top of my job was tough. I would often see Ben during the week as well, even though I needed the first couple of days to recover from the weekend (mainly the sleep deprivation). Each working week, by about Wednesday night, I would start looking forward to Friday afternoons, and seeing him again.

The university provides a professional counselling assistance program for its staff, and so it was that Ben and I found ourselves in the office of one of the psychologists, as part of a process of anger management we both agreed we needed. That counsellor did much to help Ben and me. I think he was telling the truth when he said that the father-son bond he saw between us was the strongest that he had seen in his work. We dealt with the anger. I managed to get some extra carer help, and the situation improved dramatically. As my mother used to say, it is a shame to see so much parental energy going on routine tasks that carers can do, because it cuts down so dramatically on having the energy to make the most of the other times, even if it is just the time to sit and talk over a coffee, or watch the passing parade of life.

Ben and I saw this counsellor several times, and we did manage to put in place some mutually beneficial anger management. It was in that office that Ben's and my relationship entered its final phase: a phase of calm, good humour, mutual respect and simple honesty.

I have always believed that anger is a form of concealed, repressed or unresolved sadness – a sadness so unbearable that the mind instantly transforms it into a more easily expelled, outwardly directed, emotion. I know my anger helping Ben with his daily needs was a thinly disguised mask – a mask that distracted me from the sadness and futility I felt.

Our discussions in the counsellor's office about anger led quickly into deeper waters, at least for me. One day, I was suddenly overwhelmed with all the sadness I felt about Ben's condition, and what it meant for both of us. I looked at Ben, and started crying as I talked. I told him how much I loved him, how much I would do for him if I could. I told him that Esther or I would instantly give up our own lives if we could save his. I told him I would be so devastated without him that I did not know how I would find the courage or the will to carry on. Ben's response to each of these dramatic, self-centred, statements was the same few words, 'I know, Dad.'

I don't know if it did Ben much good, but it helped me. I felt as if a huge burden had been lifted from my shoulders. I wanted him not just to sense my love for him, but to see and hear it, and I think he did. I had so little confidence that my own actions towards him would show him enough that I loved him, that I had to say these things. I know this also: from that day on, there was never any pretence from Ben that he and I were following the usual path, with him living to a ripe old age long after his grumpy old dad had passed away. From time to time, Ben would speak of what would happen in my life, after him. One of the things he asked was that I stay involved in the muscular dystrophy community. I promised him I would.

When we came out of the counsellor's office that afternoon, the sun was beginning to set across the city buildings, and the shadows of the many beautiful trees in the eastern Parklands were lengthening. We walked aimlessly for an hour or so in the Parklands, saying little, grateful to be alive, and to be together (I speak for myself; I think I speak for him too). I think we noticed every bird that chirruped, on that particular afternoon. A toilet stop was needed, and the thought of strangers meeting in Parklands toilets came suddenly into my head, and left again just as abruptly. If any such men had come into that toilet, they would have had a strange and confusing sight to take on board, as Ben and I got the job at hand done.

It is strange how the generations seem to repeat themselves. Is it an inevitable pattern, or what?

> Because the question for me was always whether that shape we see in our lives was there from the beginning or whether these random events are only called a pattern after the fact. (McCarthy, p. 231)

No answers in that novel, though the question gets mulled over from a dozen different angles. While I am mostly pleased that I had this emotional outpouring to my son, I am also ashamed. Ben reacted better than I did when the same things happened to me when I was young. I was a callow fifteen-year-old, about to go to boarding school. For fifteen years, I had been very close to my grandad, a stern man, an unemotional man. The night before I was to leave, I was with him when he burst into tears, and told me how lonely he was going to be when I went away. Until that moment, I don't think I had given his feelings a moment's thought. Now I was that old man. On another occasion, when I was twenty, my mother was at a very low point in her marriage to my father, the lowest point. She cried and cried, distraught, despairing, as if the God she had believed in all her life had abandoned her, and there was no hope left in the world. I failed her too, that day, in my lack of engagement in her misery. Now I was in her position too. When his turn came, Ben showed more empathy and guts than I ever did.

So, is everything for the best, or can nothing really be helped?

Victor Frankl also writes about the equivalence of big happinesses and little happinesses:

> The attempt to develop a sense of humour and to see things in a humorous light is some kind of trick learned while mastering the art of living. Yet it is possible to practice the art of living even in a concentration camp, although suffering is omnipresent. To draw an analogy: a man's suffering is similar to the behaviour of gas. If a certain quantity of gas is pumped into an empty chamber, it will fill the chamber completely and evenly, no matter how big the chamber. Thus suffering completely fills the human soul and conscious mind, no matter whether the suffering is great or little. Therefore, the 'size' of human suffering is absolutely relative.
>
> It also follows that a very trifling thing can cause the greatest of joys… (Frankl, p. 43)

I think I finally lean towards my mother's position – that everything is somehow for the best. In so many ways big and trifling, Benjamin brought me joy and made me happy.

6

Panic Attack

It was less than two weeks to Christmas 2004 – the first Christmas that we would spend as members of a family that had now shattered into sharp, broken fragments. My boss at the university had asked me to make an urgent trip to Malaysia on his behalf. The adrenalin shock of the separation several months earlier was wearing off, and being replaced by a mind-twisting sense of loss, aimlessness and loneliness. I agreed to go.

As each day passed during that Christmas/New Year period, I was less and less capable of doing what I had just done a day or week earlier – buy a fridge, sign a lease, arrange an electric bed for Benjamin, rent a hoist, and all the other things that you have to do when starting again, and you have your son with you every weekend. I agreed to go to Kuala Lumpur mainly because I was dreading the days leading up to this Christmas, and any distraction was welcome. I didn't want to actually move into what I thought of as my 'Mitcham motel room', even though it was a nice flat in its own right; I wanted to wake up and realise it was all a bad dream. Going to Malaysia put off the moment of truth a little longer.

I had accumulated enough frequent flyer points, so I decided to upgrade myself to business class. The first hours of the flight were uneventful. I noticed the extra frills, but I was too emotionally numb to enjoy them.

About two hours before landing in Kuala Lumpur, my problems began. I felt a sudden onset of extreme panic. I have had several panic attacks in my life. The first occurred in a school chapel when I was fifteen years old, while I was reading out the evening prayers. The feelings of terror, public embarrassment, sheer desperation at not being able to speak or breathe – these are difficult feelings to ever erase from memory. Most people, including me, who have had a panic attack would go to extreme lengths to avoid another one.

So there I am in my comfortable business class seat, suddenly overwhelmed by extreme feelings of panic and claustrophobia. I've got to get out of this confined space, this aluminium and plastic coffin, but at an altitude of 39,000 feet, this is not really an option. The metal cylinder that is the fuselage of the plane feels like a contracting iron vice, squeezing the air out of my lungs. The engine noise becomes unbearably loud. At the same time, a black liquid seems to have begun spreading from and through my insides, blotting out all my usual bodily networks, and ransacking my normal nervous systems and controls. It is this pincer-like, simultaneous onset of external threat with inner meltdown which I find the most dreadful and disabling aspect of a panic attack. The irresistible force of the external threat merges with the immovable reality of your own loss of control, destroying all semblance of your usual relatively confident self. And it all happens within seconds, and without warning.

What did I do? I sat it out, as best I could, concentrating on only one thing – my breathing, in and out, as calmly as I could manage. Within fifteen minutes, the worst was over. My normal 'self' had more or less returned, albeit highly shaken up.

In the weeks that followed, I learned a lot more from my doctor about panic attacks. Now I can see more clearly what was happening on the plane. I was getting advance warning that I was on the verge of a serious emotional collapse. Within a couple of weeks, I would have been no more capable of getting on a plane to Kuala Lumpur than flying to the moon.

For me, it was intolerably sad that Christmas Day 2004 would not be spent as a family, or even a semblance of a family. At least a few minutes when it would be just the four of us. For so long, it had been the four of us against the world, one for all and all for one. We had faced off so many challenges. Christmas Day had been spent in so many different places. Kids think Christmas is about them, and I suppose it is. What the kids don't know is how much pleasure their parents are getting through them on that day.

Anyway, I did my job for the university, and kept my scheduled appointments in the days leading up to Christmas. My flight back did not leave until late on Christmas Eve, so I had nearly a whole day with nothing much to do. I spent most of Christmas Eve that year walking aimlessly around the salubrious KLCC shopping centre underneath the Petronas Towers. I don't think I had ever felt so lonely or disconnected. Every Christmas decoration seemed to mock my state of mind. Little did I know that I had just met, the day before, the woman who was to become my second chance at love. Our first meeting was tense and unfriendly, and gave no sign of what would develop a year or more later. Indeed, after that initial meeting in her office, I had fired an email back to my colleagues recommending caution in any business dealings with what I described then as an academic 'cowgirl'.

(I am writing these words more than three years later. That 'cowgirl' has now become my greatest emotional support in life, and listens to me read what I have written each day. I am again in Kuala Lumpur, and again within walking distance of the Suria shopping mall. I take a break from my writing, and walk back to where I spent those lonely hours on Christmas Eve 2004. I find myself drawn to the Dome – a themed café emulating something that might be found on the Left Bank in Paris. Just like I did in 2004, I sit in a wicker chair at the Dome for a long while, gazing into space. But this time, I really have only one thing on my mind: how can I do justice in words to at least some aspects of my son's life?)

Within three weeks of arriving back in Adelaide that Christmas, the acute panic I had felt on the aeroplane had settled into a more or less chronic anxiety state, in which further attacks seemed constantly imminent, but never quite happened in their full intensity. But just fearing one coming on was bad enough. And also, for the first time in my life, I experienced what it means to suffer from depression. For nearly two weeks, I found it almost impossible to get out of bed. I would struggle to rise by about 9 a.m., before lying down again on the living room couch, closing my eyes, and not being able to move again, or even think, even though I was not asleep, or able to sleep, for five or six hours. I would be dimly aware of the day's progress from the changing position of the sun's rays on the walls in the room. For ten years, I had been a resilient manager and boss, able to keep on keeping on as one office drama after another came and went. And now I couldn't get out of bed. The shame and failure I felt was overwhelming, but not strong enough to snap me out of this feeling of hopeless lethargy.

How I managed to look after Ben and his needs during that time, I do not know. Yet somehow I must have done so. The only goal I had was to survive in a well enough state from Monday to Friday to be able to look after him when the weekends came around in January/February 2005. I could not eat, and lost more than six kilos in a very short time. But I knew I had to eat, to have enough energy to look after Ben. For about ten days, I survived on bananas and ice cream. I figured they would give me at least some energy for the weekends ahead.

I started on antidepressants. After about a week on medication, I began to feel a little better. It was as if I had become a car with a dead battery, and the drugs gave my depleted cells just enough of an external charge for the car to get started again, and start recharging itself. I have come through this encounter with the black dog of depression with a greatly heightened sense of what a powerful and frightening disorder it is. I will never ever again make light of it if someone says that they are feeling so down that they are having trouble getting out of bed in the morning. The other thing I've learnt is the value of medication. I was not on it for very long – maybe three months – but I know it helped me get started again. It deadened the bad stuff enough to allow what was left of the positive stuff inside me to kick in and take over. The time seemed to come naturally when I wanted to feel the full range of emotions again, the good and the bad, and so I stopped taking them.

The kindness of strangers

My Penguin edition of *The Brothers Karamazov* is looking its age. It was printed in 1972, so it is a fair bet that I read it in that year or fairly soon after. Its pages are yellowed and brittle, but it is still quite legible. It is one of those books it is easy to recommend when you get asked questions like, 'You've read a lot of books. What is the greatest novel you have ever read?' I used to think that only social groups had things like 'received opinions' – blind beliefs and prejudices that get trotted out, devoid of any real analysis of the topic at hand. I'm now more conscious that individuals develop their own set of idiosyncratic 'received opinions' – opinions that they once held with some conviction, but which have not been updated with the benefit of new knowledge for years, perhaps for decades. Because I used to say *The Brothers Karamazov* when asked such a question thirty years ago, I probably still would, without thinking about it. It's just one part of me that has become a 'received opinion,' sitting there dead and inert in my brain – a stagnant thought, not the result of any strenuous mental updating since the time the opinion was first formed, and uttered with the ignorant self-confidence of youth.

More than three years have passed since that Christmas panic attack and New Year depression I am describing here. I was at the lowest ebb of my life. Remembering those days and weeks makes me physically nauseous. Yet I somehow pulled through. How? There is a scene in Dostoevsky's novel which provides a clue to how my life worked out at that time. Mitya (one of the brothers) has been charged with the murder of his father. The police interrogation has gone on for a long time, and Mitya is utterly exhausted:

> They began working on the final draft of the official record of the evidence. Mitya got up, crossed over from his chair to the corner of the room by the curtains, lay down on the large chest covered with a rug and fell asleep at once.' (p. 595)

When he wakes, the legal process resumes, but all he can now concentrate on (especially given the intense dream he has just had) is what someone has done for him while he was asleep:

> He was suddenly struck by the fact that there was a pillow under his head, a pillow which had not been there when he sank exhausted on the chest.
>
> 'Who put that pillow under my head? Who was that kind man?' he cried with a sort of rapturous, grateful feeling and with tears in his voice, as though goodness only knows what favour has been shown him. (p. 596)

I find the page without difficulty, but not because I remember the story very well. On the contrary, I can barely remember it at all. I find the page because, in this novel of over nine hundred pages, it is the only page I marked with a pencil thirty-five years ago, when I read it for the first and only time.

I, too, experienced kindness when I most needed it and when I least expected it. Gratuitous acts of kindness, a kindness that kept my faith in human nature alive at a time when I felt I had lost everything – a secure family role, many of my friends, station in life, identity as a worthwhile human being.

Thank you, Keith. Among your many kindnesses, you prepared a special Christmas lunch for me that year, which the two of us ate sitting at your little table in your kitchen, before we both spent time with our children later in the day.

Thank you, Jane. You took a day off work and invited me on a picnic. I told you beforehand that I was not up to anything, not even talking. You said you would organise it all. I remember spending most of the afternoon lying on a rug on the banks of the River Torrens, incapable of sustained conversation, staring up at the leaves on the gum trees above.

Thank you, Rod. You flew from Sydney when my depression was deepest. You spent nearly a week in my flat, making cups of tea, reading *The Shipping News*, and listening sympathetically when I would stir for a few moments and talk about how I felt my life had ended in failure.

And thank you to a long-dead Russian novelist. You gave me Mitya and his reaction to gratuitous acts of kindness as a telling frame of reference early on in my life, and it stood me in good stead when I needed it most decades later.

The first weeks and months living in my self-declared Mitcham motel room were not encouraging, but those acts of kindness were also telltale signs that all was not lost, that it was time to start picking up the pieces and getting on with the new realities I had to live by.

Benjamin was with me every weekend through all of this, coping as best he could with his own tsunami of anxieties and sorrows. Though we talked about many things, discussing my failed marriage with him was out of the question: though twenty years of age, he was totally reliant on both of his parents all of the time for the basics of existence. He loved both of us unconditionally and with total loyalty. The rupture in his parents' relationship and his family life was on stark display every week as he and his van load of necessary gear was transferred from one parent's place to the other. Any previous comfort or sense of identity that he got from being a member of a happy family was now non-existent, had been undeniably obliterated. For years we had been two goldfish in a glass fishbowl, swimming happily in that watery ethos called family. The bowl had been smashed, the water had gone everywhere, and we were floundering around in the broken glass, needing to change into something else, and needing it fast.

We were both faced with having to leave many precious things behind, and to go forward into a new stage of life. And slowly but surely, we did so; we started to build a new kind of relationship together.

When it came time to find somewhere to live, I had picked the suburb of Mitcham for a mixture of practical and sentimental reasons. A practical reason was to do with location – halfway between Magill, where I worked, and Glenelg, the family home (not sold at that point). But just as important was another consideration. It was an area Ben was very familiar with – within walking distance of his two schools (Mitcham Primary and Unley High), and close to a pub (the

Edinburgh) where kids he knew from school might hang out. The flat I rented was midway between the 'Ed' and the more downmarket Torrens Arms, or 'TA', the other pub in Mitcham, and we made many outings to both pubs – to play the pokies, to have a glass of wine (well, I drank the wine while Ben had a diet Coke), or a cheap bar meal. The Ed had an implausibly cheap mixed grill, which they did away with a few weeks after we took a liking to it. The TA had their own version, called a Truckstop: sausages, bacon, fried egg, lots of gravy, all on top of a mound of mashed potato, and a generous Greek side salad in an extra bowl.

At first, I had extreme difficulty adapting to my changed circumstances and station in life. I had been in a relationship for twenty-three years, a family man for twenty years, the owner of a comfortable 'character' house in a salubrious seaside suburb for thirteen years, and head of a large university department for over ten years. And all these roles ended, seemingly in the blink of an eye, within a few weeks of each other. In retrospect, I had obviously sensed that change was coming. Six months earlier, less than a month after Ben had finished at Unley High School, I had submitted my resignation as head of department. I could see that such a high-pressure job was going to be incompatible with Ben's new situation in life, now that he had been disgorged from the structure (the school system) that had organised his daily life for twelve years. Everything was going to be different for him from now on, and for us, now that he was not going to be picked up every school day at 8 a.m. in an access cab, and dropped off at 4.30 each afternoon.

Now I was living a few blocks from those same schools. In those first few months, there were many evenings when I feared facing my flat alone and, on my way home, I stopped off at the bar of the Torrens Arms for a glass of red or white. I would look across the road at the laundromat on Belair Road where I did my weekly washing. A Hopperesque symbol, I thought, for my new status in life.

Mitcham is not a suburb any sane person would normally associate with Edward Hopper. It is a suburb with many attractive features, designed to cater to the needs and aspirations of a mildly professional man (comfortably off, but not ostentatiously rich), and his family. The fabled nuclear family survives in Mitcham, not so much as a demographic reality but as a ubiquitous sign of what it means to be happy and normal in life, including living in a house of your own, on tree-lined streets. Our wheelchair-accessible van was too big for my garage, so I had to park it on the street. An apt commentary on my falling status, I felt. Not being able to give my vehicle a proper, off-street home for the night either. My luck with the nuclear family had well and truly run out, it seemed.

The only constant in my life for those first few months was my son, combined with an occasional visit from my daughter, who would bring a few of her things with her, enough to make the spare room seem like hers, and who would cheer me up immensely when she came to sleep over. I was not just happy to see her, I was grateful.

My self-pity seemed grandiose, even to myself at the time. I had become unaccommodated man. I did not think I had any more layers left to lose. I was both right and wrong on this point. If Ben had died at that time, I would have been in much worse shape than I was. Thankfully, he didn't. And so, gradually, I came to stop being obsessed with what I had lost, or trying to make sense of it, and started to rebuild some kind of life for myself.

I can barely imagine what it must have been like for Ben through all this, being passed backwards and forwards between his tense parents like a hot potato. He did his best to make these early handovers, which were handled almost all the time with a civil if not polite efficiency, as free of stress as possible. But he suffered. He would often cry at those points, sitting in his wheelchair chained into the van, packed in around all his necessary goods and chattels (bedding, clothing, toilet chair, breathing machine, chargers and so on), having to say goodbye to his mother or his father.

But even in those first grim weeks, we had some great times. We were discovering that we actually liked one another's company, not as father and son, not as members of a family, but as two blokes who now had plenty of time to just hang out together. Sunday afternoons walking around Mitcham, exploring the environs of Brownhill Creek, making wagers with each other on when the rains would come and the creek would start to flow again, having makeshift picnics in the local parks, catching the bus into the city, watching the excavations progress for the new Mitcham shopping mall, visiting the local pubs.

As a son, Benjamin was always there for me, and me for him, from the moment he was born; but as 'single' mates and friends, we somehow reinvented each other from scratch, at a time when we had to. Our conversation would be constant, it would cover a multitude of topics, it would rarely touch on sensitive topics to do with his parents' relationship (and if it did, never in such a way to blame or criticise either parent), but everything else was up for discussion. He did a brilliant job of defending the honour, so to speak, of both his mother and his father. And yet I am sure he also knew how difficult it must have been for his parents to maintain much of a relationship while looking after him. Every now and again, he would make some comment to that effect. He was smart enough to understand the stress that a disabled child puts on a marriage.

My first few months at Mitcham, and the weekends with my son. Those weekends, when it was just the two of us, quickly became the centre of my life. Our beds were within touching distance in the same small room; we got into our pattern of long talks after finally getting settled into bed, talks which continued right up until the last weekend of his life. I loved hearing his voice, listening to the curiosity or spirit of enquiry in his voice, asking me what I thought on obscure topics (as if I would know!), the 'Goodnight, Ben, I love you. Goodnight, Dad, luv ya' routines, and then when he was asleep, falling asleep myself to the sound of his bi-pap breathing apparatus – part human, part machine. Such was my peace of mind when he was there breathing in the same room that, although there were many nights when I didn't get enough sleep, there was never a night when I couldn't sleep because of worries or anxieties. Knowing he was there, a few metres away, sleeping peacefully – that was the best possible sleeping pill for me.

My mother once said that the happiest moments of her life were when her children were young and they were all safe and sound at home. I can vouch for that. I never felt more secure or at peace than those nights when I had my son sleeping in my room.

Ben used to joke about it being our bachelors' pad. But things change; I eventually bought another house, a much more modest one, in a much more modest suburb. Rosanna moved back in with me. Our days as two bachelors sharing our pad were over. He and I both enjoyed having Rosanna back.

In one of his essays, Walter Benjamin writes about the ephemerality of the remembered past, no matter how intensely it has been recollected:

> Reminiscences, even extensive ones, do not always amount to an autobiography. For autobiography has to do with time, with sequence, and what makes up the continuous flow of life. Here, I am talking of a space, of moments and discontinuities. For even if months and years appear here, it is in the form they have in the moment of recollection. This strange form – it may be called fleeting or eternal – is in neither case the stuff that life is made of. (Benjamin, p. 612)

I spent a total of twenty months in my Mitcham unit. I was away from the flat for five or six weekends, some of them with Ben, so Ben must have spent about seventy-five weekends there with me. I was only in my new house for a year before he died. He was in hospital for a month of that time, so he probably spent about half as many weekends with me in my new house as he did in my Mitcham flat. These figures shock me now. It feels the opposite: the good and bad times in Mitcham being over in a flash, and the recovery period in 'our' new house, when I had got both of my children back as a 'family' under my roof, going on almost forever.

7

From Son to Mate, and Back Again

'You've lost your mate,' a woman I hardly knew said to me at Ben's funeral. She was a carer who had been with him when he collapsed, the last person he had spoken to. She had only known Ben for a little over a week, but whatever he had said to her about me, or she had worked out for herself from the few times she had seen us together, was enough to make her know this much about him and me.

Yes, Ben had become my mate in the years after he finished high school. We drank together, played the pokies together, watched obscure films together (for reasons unknown, Ben had developed a fascination with all things John Malkovitch), did all sorts of things together. His voice and thoughts became the soundtrack to much of my life, just as mine must have become for him. We laughed at each other's witticisms, no matter how forced; I 'got' his sense of humour, and the world it came from.

This mateship had its limits. More than once, he made it clear to me that, no matter how much I thought we were good mates, I had to remember that I was his fallback position; that he would have preferred to have more mates his own age, that I was a very feeble substitute for a sexual relationship with a girl (something he craved, but never had). I wasn't convinced about the age thing, but I could hardly deny that he might find a young woman his age more pleasurable company than a grumpy old dad pushing sixty.

Boxing Day 2004

Benjamin and I are driving from Adelaide to Melbourne for a week's holiday. As a family, we used to take lots of holidays like this. He and I were continuing the tradition, even if the model of a family unit we knew best was now in tatters. (When the break-up came, Esther and I were no more able to find common ground in a common language than if she had been speaking in Schweitzerdeutsch and me in Gaelic.) Through the Muscular Dystrophy Association in Victoria, I had been able to obtain accessible accommodation at a nice hotel on Southbank, one block back from the Yarra, and that was where we were now headed. Ben knew his way around the CBDs of Melbourne and Sydney like he knew his way around Adelaide.

On that familiar journey, I was putting petrol in the tank at Bordertown (where we had spent our first night in South Australia fourteen years earlier, in 1990) when a newsflash came over the radio, about a large tidal wave affecting parts of Indonesia and Thailand. That was the first we heard of the Boxing Day tsunami. The closer we got to Melbourne that day, the more prominent that news item became. By the time we had checked into the hotel and turned on Sky *News*, the full scale of the devastation was becoming evident. We spent six days in and out of that hotel room, watching the death toll estimates rising every time we turned on the television set.

Ben and I had many great times on that trip. It would take us until at least 1 or 2 p.m. to be ready to leave the hotel room, but then we would be out for the next ten hours or so, getting back around 10 or 11 p.m., then two hours to get to bed, then sleeping until 10 a.m. or so. On most days, I would find a public park and have a rest on the grass, catching up from my broken sleep, while he went off exploring the local neighbourhood.

We went to Williamstown by train and Port Melbourne by tram, in each place finding a bar near the waterfront with an ambience we both liked. I would have a glass of white wine while Ben sipped on his diet Coke, and we shared some snack like garlic bread. Sitting on the dock of the bay, just watching the tide roll by. Times like this, times when being trumps doing. A favourite café in Federation Square also became a focal point for doing nothing much, enjoyably.

It was the best of times and the worst of times. I very much enjoyed those long periods of time when it was just the two of us, out exploring the city. We were both curious creatures, even if not always curious about the same things. We had a similar tendency to postulate pointless structures out of the formlessness of events, as in seeing how many minutes it took to cover a certain number of city blocks, or tallying up how many disabled spaces were provided in different car parks. We would talk, but not constantly. There were many times when I would be lost in my own thoughts, and Ben would be observing some aspect of his environment and forming speculations about it that he would then bring up and ask me for my opinion. Some of these things I would have no ability to comment on sensibly, such as whether the road workers were doing it the best way or not, or why a certain street sign seemed to make no sense.

I now know, however, what I could not face up to then: that Benjamin was damaged by the family break-up just as I was. What I am less sure about is whether there was any other way he and I could have developed the adult friendship we did. He suffered a lot because his parents no longer wanted to be together, but he and I also gained a lot in terms of our own relationship with each other. Neither of us could borrow any longer from the collective family capital to shore up our own individual identities. He now had a relationship with his mother, a relationship with me, and one with his sister, and none of them overlapped. I no longer had my relationship with him mediated through his mother. Of course, he was also twenty years of age, and intensively (and necessarily) dependent on both his parents – something completely alien for most sons that age. Rosanna, though two years younger, had turned to her peers for her identity, and away from her family, years earlier. Ben could not do the same.

So, yes, it was the best of times and the worst of times. Of the overarching marble structure that had given meaning, security and comfort to our lives for so long, a huge central chunk had come crashing down. We both had to find a new role, a new identity, and so it was that Ben became my friend when I most needed one, and I became his friend when he needed one too. These new identities were quickly forming when we were on this 2004 trip to Melbourne together, and remained central to both our lives for the next two and a half years.

The gains were real, but did not completely disguise how real the losses were too. One evening, we were on the footpath outside Flinders Street railway station. We had just eaten in a cheap Indian restaurant, and were on our way back to the hotel on the other side of the Yarra.

Without warning, Benjamin stopped moving forward in his chair, in the middle of a busy footpath, and began to weep. Huge tears flowed down his cheeks, noisy sobs came from his chest. Passers-by scurried past, averting their gazes as much as they could. Confronting enough to see a severely disabled young man in a wheelchair; so much more so when he is weeping inconsolably. Now, years later, it is painful for me to recall this scene; my breathing is becoming fast and shallow as the panic rises. I cannot bear to think that he spent a single minute of his short life so sad and unhappy that he would need to sob like that, unable to do anything about drawing attention to his abject self on this busy Melbourne street.

Standing next to him as the evening crowds rushed into Flinders Street station, feeling utterly helpless, wanting to comfort him, but knowing there was nothing I could do, in desperation I decided to ring Esther on my mobile. For the next ten minutes, I held the phone next to his ear, while she calmly talked to him, and he listened carefully. (I remember this detail in particular – he really paid close attention to every word she was saying to him.) I learned a lesson that night. In Ben's case, no matter how well he got on with me, it was his mother who gave him that existential sense of security that comforted and protected him when he was most afraid. On many nights over the years of his growing up, she was the one able to take him to a safe place when he was frightened, and she succeeded again that night. The tears dried up; the distress passed.

> The word goes round Repins,
> the murmur goes round Lorenzinis,
> at Tattersalls, men look up from sheets of numbers,
> the Stock Exchange scribblers forget the chalk in their hands
> and men with bread in their pockets leave the Greek Club:
> There's a fellow crying in Martin Place. They can't stop him.
> The traffic in George Street is banked up for half a mile
> and drained of motion. The crowds are edgy with talk
> and more crowds come hurrying. Many run in the back streets
> which minutes ago were busy main streets, pointing:
> There's a fellow weeping down there. No one can stop him.

And so Ben has his 'Les Murray' moment, albeit in Melbourne rather than Sydney. Murray's poem goes on,

> but the weeping man, like the earth, requires nothing,
> the man who weeps ignores us, and cries out
> of his writhen face and ordinary body
> not words, but grief, not messages, but sorrow
> hard as the earth, sheer, present as the sea –
> and when he stops, he simply walks between us
> mopping his face with the dignity of one
> man who has wept, and now has finished weeping.
>   (From Les A. Murray, 'An Absolutely Ordinary Rainbow')

There was a time when I was a young tutor, and used to grade hundreds of Year 12 students' annual attempts to read this poem in the light of one essay question or another set for them in an English exam. There was a time when the meaning of the poem seemed easy enough to grasp, at least in broad outline. There also came a time, this time, when Les Murray's poem made complete existential sense to me, and I knew that I had known almost nothing worth knowing about the poem, or about tears, before that night in Flinders Street. That night,

Ben made his way back to our hotel, his wet face mopped and dried, bearing the dignity of a man who had wept, and had now finished weeping.

A history of tears. A tsunami of tears. Every time I visit Ben's final resting place in Centennial Park, I cry. From time to time I have to stop writing this story because I can no longer clearly see the keyboard. I have learnt a lot about tears. They are not all the same; they are never far away. Is it possible to construct a taxonomy of tears, of weeping? Roland Barthes asked himself such questions,.

> Who will write the history of tears? In which societies, in which periods, have we wept? Since when is it that men (and not women) no longer cry? (Barthes, p. 427)

Barthes answers his own questions by noting that weeping is a social act – the person crying is communicating with someone, perhaps even with other parts of their own self:

> ... I make myself cry, in order to prove to myself that my grief is not an illusion: tears are signs, not expressions. By my tears, I tell a story, I produce a myth of grief, and henceforth I adjust myself to it: I can live with it, because, by weeping, I give myself the 'truest' of messages, that of my body, not that of my speech: 'Words, what are they? One tear will say more than all of them.' (Barthes, p. 428)

I had been powerless to help Ben. I should have known better. Four years earlier, I had been that weeping man.

On 15 July 2000, I had also been on a plane to Kuala Lumpur. The day before, Ben had carried the Olympic torch through the streets of northern Adelaide. The preceding months of that year had been tumultuous, beginning in February with a major operation that had fused his spine with two long metal rods, and leading up to this high point in Ben's life, when he had been a proud torchbearer and privileged participant in this leg of the Sydney Olympics. Under the leaden grey skies that afternoon, the day before my flight, something cracked in me, as surely as if it had been a timber joist holding up a floor. I was full of conflicted emotions about Ben and his life, and therefore mine, emotions that I had been holding in for many years. That afternoon, watching him pressing one hand around that torch, while steering his chair past the excited, cheering crowd with the other, something in me gave way, something slipped.

A day later, on the plane trip from Adelaide to Malaysia, I started to weep. All of a sudden. Without warning. In place of the men from Tattersalls or the Stock Exchange, my passers-by were the Malaysian cabin crew, doing their best not to notice.

I have often thought about that flight, and my own tsunami of tears. But Barthes' words give me pause. Am I inventing my own myth of grief, after the event? Why was I crying? Twenty-four hours earlier, Ben had had one of the greatest days of his life. Perhaps that was the key – the heightening of emotions associated with my son, albeit in a transcendent, happy way? Had it taken a once-in-a-lifetime ecstatic experience to dislodge the feelings of grief that I had blocked for so long? Could it be possible that the many low points in the story of his disease were so low that I couldn't really grieve, and then still function effectively in making the most of a bad situation, and just get on with it, stressing to myself and to others the silver lining that the grey clouds brought with them, no matter how dark the silver?

The day of the Olympic torch relay was a turning point for me, as I found out on the plane the next day. The progress of Ben's disease was taking an emotional toll. What it was slowly becoming was now undeniable in its impact. The elephant in the room was rampaging all over the familiar furniture. After the emotional breakdown on that plane, my reactions had become unhinged from solid supports or reference points. I was no longer holding my feelings together very well. Even if it was not yet apparent to most of the people around me, it was obvious to me.

A few lines in *The Spanish Tragedy* could have been written about Duchenne muscular dystrophy:

> And so it grew and grew
> And bore and bore
> Until at length it
> Grew a gallows that did bear our son.

Still, the Sydney Olympics came and went, life went on, and that Melbourne trip four years later, during the 2004 tsunami, was a happy interlude between a grim previous few months and an even grimmer few weeks of depression to come. In Melbourne that Christmas, I enjoyed Ben's company, and he enjoyed mine. We moved at a similar pace through experiences, like going along city streets or through arcades or parks. Neither of us seemed to get impatient with the other to move on. We both found the world a curious, fascinating place, which we enjoyed turning into talk.

One afternoon, we were at a wheelchair-accessible tram stop in front of Federation Square. A tram to St Kilda was approaching. Recklessly, I told Ben to get on, and then got on myself.

I assumed that an important destination like St Kilda would have a wheelchair-accessible platform. If it didn't, I assumed the tram would simply reverse its route back into the city, and we would get off where we got on. Wrong, on both counts. As we pulled into St Kilda, no sign of a ramp to get off. Then the route number was changed. The tram was not coming back into the city. We would be stuck on this tram, because it would be impossible for Ben in his wheelchair to get off. What if the tram was going to the Kew depot? It would be almost impossible to get off there, without a forklift. What if he needed a toilet stop? (This was at a time when he was experiencing extreme anxiety about urination issues, and was convinced for days and weeks at a time that he had wet himself, and that everyone could see a wet patch on his pants and chair.) I held my breath, hoping the final destination was not too far away, and that Ben could 'last' for all this extra, unanticipated time. We got a great tour of the leafy eastern suburbs of Melbourne, before we eventually got back to our original stop nearly three hours after we boarded that tram. Being stuck on a tram to nowhere with Ben needing to go to the toilet (with all the coordination and work that that entailed) would not have been a relaxing experience.

Most of the things we did with Ben were planned and followed through with military precision. They had to be. The consequences of failure were so high. But that did not stop me doing some rash things with him over the years. Nor did he need much encouragement to join in, being more of a gutsy risk-taking adventurer than I could ever be.

Ben's courage in everyday situations was so ordinary it was easy to overlook. Many times in Adelaide, he caught trains on his own, relying on the driver to put a ramp down for him, and to remember which station he had to stop the train at. A small thing? Yes and no. My fear was that a wheel of his chair would get caught in the deep grooves running alongside the actual railway tracks as he was exiting the station on the pedestrian walkways. There was no way he could have got himself out of that groove, and out of the path of oncoming trains. It had happened to one of his mates, who had been extricated without incident by a passer-by. One of the 'wheelies' in Peter Rose's memoir about his brother was not so lucky, and was killed by an oncoming train when his chair got caught in just such a groove.

So, Ben catching trains on his own? Yes, I call that courage.

Family, culture, religion

My kids were brought up in a secular household. In our years in Glenelg, we were not churchgoers. Benjamin went to Unley High School by necessity (for the extra resources and support provided), while Rosanna went to nearby Brighton High School by choice. We did not want our kids educated in church schools.

Religion did not figure prominently in Ben's life, except for two periods when he wanted us to take him to Sunday Mass: the first when he was around ten years of age; and the second nearly a decade later when his parents separated. On both occasions, I think he wanted to see if religion could offer him any answers to the grim situation he found himself in. On both occasions, I think the conclusion he reached after a few months was that he wasn't going to find any answers inside a church. His view firmed as he got older.

He surprised me one day when, out of the blue, he said something like, 'We are being asked to believe that God is all-loving and all-powerful…and he allows diseases like muscular dystrophy to exist in the world…' and then he just chuckled to himself and said no more, his unfinished sentence confirming that the absurdity of such a proposition must be self-evident to any rational human being. On this point, at least, I tend to agree with him. I become annoyed when well-meaning people say that he must have been on this earth with this particular condition for a reason. It was even put to me once in its most extreme and offensive form: we choose our disease; Ben had chosen to have muscular dystrophy.

And yet there is one undeniable truth about Ben's more recent experiences of religion: he gained comfort and meaning from going to church. In our case, this church-going took the form of Sunday 6 p.m. Mass at St Francis Xavier's Cathedral in Victoria Square, in the centre of Adelaide. And the truth is that I did too, even though I had as much doubt as he did about the central tenets of the Christian faith, as passed down to us by our forebears.

My mother, fervent Catholic though she is, once pointed out just one of the many absurdities that believers are asked to take some comfort in. Heaven, for example, and the hope we have of meeting our loved ones there again after we have died. The need to believe this is desperate when you are mourning their loss. I would do anything if it meant that I was going to get my boy back after I die, and that we could pick up our rapport where we left off on the night he died. Mum is eighty years old; her mother died aged thirty-two when Mum was an eight-year-old girl. 'Imagine what that reunion is going to be like,' she said. 'My mother, a young slip of a woman, coming face to face with her old daughter, fifty years older than her, and both of us picking up where we left off seventy years ago. Heaven can't possibly be like that.'

Religion gives me comfort, even strength, yet assaults my rationality; Ben and I both gained peace and some sense of identity greater than ourselves when we went to Mass during the last few years of his life. Being part of a community may be one aspect of it. At least for me, I became open to the possibility that I had seriously misunderstood, or underestimated, three big aspects of my upbringing: family, culture, and religion. And Ben, and going to Mass with him, played a direct role in this re-evaluation, which is why I am writing about it here.

It interested and amused me to see the way that Ben felt he had a right to take communion, even though the only prerequisite Catholic ritual he had been through was to be baptised, in the same church I was, when he was three years old. (The old priest, a friend of the family, performed Ben's and his sister's christening without asking any of the questions he was supposed to ask, or concerning himself with the fact that we parents had not had a Catholic wedding.)

What does it mean to say that a church or a religion is bigger than ourselves? Barack Obama, writing about the role of church in the poor parts of Chicago, makes a telling point in his memoir. He captures beautifully how a community can be held together by religion when nearly everything else is failing. A gathering in a church, and then the remembrance after death, can provide a community of last resort, so to speak.

Self-evidently, religion, like language, is a social fact. What I see more clearly now is that religion is not an individual thing; it is not a personally embraced hobby or avocation like gardening, or a passionate interest in Mahler, or any other individual construct. It is a complex structure of feelings and ideas, formed over centuries, influenced by millions of lives, an evolved reality with all that this implies about very long time frames and innumerable instances of learning from trial and error. It makes no more sense, at least for me, to think of religion as an individual thing than to think one person could single-handedly write the computer programs for Microsoft or

Google, or build a pyramid. It is more complex than any one person can possibly comprehend, or for that matter plausibly refute. I've realised that the consolations of the religion I was brought up in can still apply, irrespective of belief in any particular tenets of that faith. Ben helped get me to this place, because an important part of how I got there was with and through him. I saw him get there.

Sceptics might scoff that I would say that, wouldn't I? I have lost a son. He and I were the exception, not the rule, in terms of our mutual neediness. I once thought like that. Religion is the opiate of the masses. What has changed for me is that I now think the grieving self is the rule, for all of us, sooner or later. There is a need for this kind of drug while we love and our loved ones die.

And religion is also the club where the dead remain just as much active and paid-up members as the living. Listen to the references to the dead in any Catholic Mass. There are many. Ben is not an afterthought while I am in a church; he is there, willed there and spoken about by the community that sustains that church. We are allowed to treat the dead as still with us when we are in a church.

Aussie mates

In the years after he finished high school, Ben and I became mates – Aussie mates. He was brought up in Australia, and thought of himself as proudly Australian. If he had been brought up in Switzerland or America (his other two nationalities), then I am sure he would have thought of himself as Swiss or American, to the same degree as he felt an Aussie. This was a lucky break for me. Firstly, I was Australian too, and shared the culture that Ben was completely at home in. Secondly, my times with him made me more aware than I have ever been in my life that sharing a popular culture is important.

Isabel Allende made this comment about exile from one's home culture when interviewed by Andrew Denton:

> I had lost…my country. Your country is the place where you don't have to ask. You know the code, you know the clues, you know the

jokes, you have the references, you get the accent... You only have that in your own country and of course I lost it when I left Chile. (Andrew Denton, transcript from 30 June 2008 program)

The religion and culture of your childhood? Your family roots? None of these seemed particularly important to me for quite some time. University had taken me to universalistic worlds far removed from these three (atavistic? reactionary?) frames of reference. Interesting friends and stimulating colleagues had replaced extended family in my daily interactions. The only family that mattered was my own nuclear family, and for a time it seemed sufficient. However, *in extremis*, it wasn't enough, and, as Peter Rose noted about a time of intense crisis in his own family, consolations become more primitive. Rose quotes the writer Robert McCrum to make his point. McCrum is recovering in hospital after a stroke:

> The more I stayed helpless in hospital, the more I came to understand why it is our blood relations who will respond, instinctively and without question, to the claims of family. I had lived in a world seemingly outside family, but there were moments during those first hospital days when it seemed that family was the only world that mattered... If I were now to reduce my experience in hospital to two key words they would be 'family' and 'love'. (McCrum, quoted in Rose, p. 114)

Blood relations, people who look a bit like you, who are quite a lot like you, matter, whether it is at funerals or in courtrooms. Even the worst offending criminals more often than not have some family members present when they are sentenced. I now understand why. That so many of my family made the effort (considerable effort in some cases) to get to Ben's funeral was incredibly important to me.

What am I trying to say here? In the last few paragraphs, I have been flailing around, desperately jumping from Barack Obama (on the consolations of religion) to Isabel Allende (on the consolations of one's own national culture) to Robert McCrum (on the consolations of family). What I am trying to say is this: I made these late discoveries, not on my own, not in the abstract, not as an individual decision or lifestyle choice, but socially, through shared experiences with my son.

Religion, culture, family: for much of my adult life, these were unexamined and mostly unneeded preludes to the life I was living (as an academic, as a parent, as part of the disability world). But my son's life is empirical fact. When we were at Mass, we felt simultaneously both together with one another, and at home within a community of strangers living and dead; when we were part of the roar of the crowd when Glenn McGrath took a wicket, we felt the same thing – part of something that was around when Bradman went out to bat, and would be around after we were dead; when we were playing blackjack or poker with his sister or his uncles, we felt this same sense of belonging somewhere. In each case, this home was distantly familiar to me; it was a surviving simulacrum of my own prehistory. It was less Ben's past, but still it had become 'really real' for us both. How can I explain this? All I can do is to take note, record my gratitude that I ever had these shared experiences with Ben, and leave the reader to reach their own conclusions about the mystery that is each of these things: our family, our culture, our childhood religion.

8

Losing Ben

For reasons that couldn't be helped and perhaps were also for the best, the last six weeks of Benjamin's life were spent in two places: at the Julia Farr Centre in Adelaide (formerly known as the 'Home for the Incurables') on week nights, where he was officially classified as 'on respite'; and with me as usual at my place on the weekends, as well as most weekday afternoons and evenings.

The first five of those six weeks were spent in the Huntington's ward, accommodation for a dozen or so people (sufferers? clients? residents?), where Ben shared a room with a middle-aged man named Paul. Typically hospital ward in design, these rooms had been these people's homes for decades, as well as for rest of their lives. What goes around comes around. The uncle of one of my closest colleagues had been a manager at the Julia Farr Centre once, living in his own imposing residence in the park-like grounds. After a stroke, he went from superintendent to permanent resident for the rest of his days.

Huntington's disease. The word made me shudder before I knew anything about it, before I got to see what life was like inside a 'Huntington's ward', and the fear is no less now. In most hospital or nursing home environments, intensive care units excepted, there seems to be some sort of constant droll chit-chat going on between patients/residents and staff. Not so in a Huntington's ward, if this one was typical. In my five weeks of visiting daily, I did not hear a single word uttered by any of the residents, although it was still a fairly noisy place, with jarring sounds coming from vocal chords or the crashing movements of bodies, chairs and beds.

Huntington's disease, like muscular dystrophy, is one of the many strange diseases, genetic in origin, that have been plotted and catalogued since the late nineteenth century. Among its many signature traits are jerky, random and uncontrollable movements, loss of meaningful facial expression, and other extremely debilitating physical effects, destroying continence, chewing and swallowing, and mobility. Psychological symptoms include anxiety, depression and aggression. Strange long-term diseases like these are living narratives, each with their own strong storyline; each of them with lots of individual variations which seem dramatic at the time but which fizzle out as the main plot of the disease, encoded as it is in the very DNA of the protagonist, sooner or later reaches its destined end, an end with sentiments in common with a Shakespearian tragedy: horror, death and suffering, but, for those not directly involved, a certain balance returning to the world as the normal emphatically reasserts itself.

No human being needs to read horror stories when any medical encyclopaedia will provide more unnerving disruption to what is familiar and comforting about our human nature than any sane person could possibly want. Huntington's disease and Duchenne muscular dystrophy are bad enough, but by no means exhaust the range of the possible. San Filippo syndrome, for instance, is one particularly terrible and bizarre disease/story I recently learned about. San Fillippo somehow manages to combine the worst of Huntington's with the worst of muscular dystrophy. No mean feat.

Benjamin was obviously in the wrong place, a fish out of water, a displaced person, a complete anomaly, in the Huntington's ward. I don't think the authorities believed for one moment that this was the best social place for someone with his condition. He was just as physically helpless as his fellow residents in the Huntington's community, maybe even more so, but he had control of words and concepts, like being able to let the staff know if the room was on fire or not, or being able to answer if asked whether he wanted something to eat or drink. He knew if he needed to go to the toilet, and he knew what it would be like to have an accident. But most of all, there was his instinctive chattiness and good humour. Even with strangers, he would more often than not take the lead in making conversation. So why was he assigned to a place where he was the only one who could talk? Of course there is a certain logic to most things a system does, even if it means taking away your gold teeth before gassing you. Of course the authorities also had to manage the deployment of their own limited resources; putting Ben in such a high-dependency ward was a risk management strategy, one way of decreasing the likelihood that his high level of physical needs would lead to some kind of accident or disaster.

Psychologically and socially, the Huntington's ward was a daunting, fearful and dull place for him to be. Someone must have noticed, because he was eventually offered a room of his own in another ward on one of the top floors, from where he could see the sun set across the St Vincent Gulf, and also, in the middle distance, the Glenelg seashore – the pine-studded seaside where he had spent so many happy hours, days and years of his childhood.

The day came for the move. As we left the Huntington's ward for the last time, Ben quietly murmured a few words of goodbye to Paul, his room-mate for the previous five weeks, a middle-aged man who seemed in a fairly advanced state of the disease, sufficient to have to be physically restrained in bed at night, presumably to prevent him from unconsciously hurling himself out of it. (For such reasons, all windows were always locked in the Huntington's ward.)

Ben hesitated at the entrance to the room, just after he said goodbye to an expressionless Paul, who was tied into some sort of ungainly sitting position in a wheelchair.

'Dad, I feel bad.'

'Why's that, Ben?'

'I hope Paul doesn't feel that I'm letting him down, or hurting his feelings, by leaving him here on his own while I go off to someplace better.'

Even in this grim situation, Ben was thinking about this man's feelings, for that is exactly how he saw Paul – as another human being, part of someone's family, once someone's loved baby boy, just like us, with three or four absolutely ordinary family photos stuck on the walls with Blu-tack, with thoughts and feelings even if we had no way of knowing what those thoughts and feelings were. I did my best to reassure Ben that Paul was almost certainly not aware enough of what was going on to know if Ben was staying or going. (I don't know if this was really true. I was so focused on getting Ben into a better living space that I would have sacrificed Paul's needs for Ben's without a second thought.) But Ben thought there was a flickering consciousness there behind those expressionless but wild eyes, and he would have known this better than anyone at that time. I made light of Ben's concern then, but thinking about it now is not so easy.

If there is one memory of my son's life that I hope lives on, it is this – his compassion for Paul as he said goodbye to him for the last time, a man he had shared long, alien nights with for five weeks, a roommate not able to speak a word back to him in that whole time.

Ben moved to his new room. There were cheerful staff to talk to and residents with a wide range of personality types and correspondingly extreme behaviours. The way plates and meals used to get thrown around the 'dining room' amused Ben considerably. Compared to the Huntington's ward four floors below, it had the relaxed and cheery atmosphere of an unruly holiday resort. (Of course it was no resort. No one gets to be housed at the taxpayer's expense in a place like this unless something very serious has already gone wrong.)

He had about a week in this pleasant room. And it was in this room where his heart stopped, more or less in mid-sentence, half an hour or so after leaving my house, while chatting to the two women on duty who were preparing him for bed. I hope he was looking west at that moment. I hope the curtains of his room were open. The winter sky would have been pitch-black, but the lights of Glenelg would have been twinkling in the distance, and beyond them the dark sea. I hope the rainy night, the black sea, and the twinkling lights of his childhood home were the last things he was looking at, and maybe even thinking happy thoughts about.

> How many times do we live? How many times do we die? They say we all lose 21 grams... at the exact moment of our death. Everyone. And how much fits into 21 grams? How much is lost? When do we lose 21 grams? How much goes with them? How much is gained? Twenty-one grams. The weight of a stack of five nickels. The weight of a hummingbird. A chocolate bar. How much did 21 grams weigh? (From the *21 grams* screenplay)

Those last six weeks were bitter-sweet for me. For the first time in his life, he had achieved some real independence from his parents. I noticed that he wanted to talk to me more about sex – a sure sign that he was seeing himself less as a dependent son and more as a young man with lots of testosterone in his blood and sex on his mind. I loved the way he would tell me he was nervous about getting a hard-on when he was being 'handled' by his various female carers, who were often young women who could quite easily have been his girlfriends in different circumstances; and I know he thought that one of the women he spoke his last words to was a woman he found very attractive, even if she was nearly old enough to be his mother. (At his funeral, she was the one who simply said to me, 'You've lost your mate.')

Our weekends together had continued as usual. And he and I also quickly established a new routine for the days in between. His mother was recovering from an illness, so most of his daily care was being attended to by me with help from carers. I was on study leave from my regular job, so was more flexible in the time I could spend with him. After his first night in the Huntington's ward, I knew I had to get him out of there as much as possible. I rearranged my work routines so that he could spend every day with me, from after lunch until about 9 p.m. at night, unless there was something else he wanted to do.

I didn't know it then, but I had had a very lucky break. I got to spend nearly every day of his last six weeks with him. Even better, during the weekdays, the time I had with him was even more enjoyable, because I had had an uninterrupted sleep, in my own bed, and did not have the stressful and physically tiring work associated with getting him up in the morning or getting him to bed at night. It was pure quality time. I would do my own work in the mornings, cheerful because I had his company to look forward to later in the day. I organised my week around his routines: electric wheelchair sports on Monday, the WEA philosophy course we were doing on Tuesday, his volunteer work with the Muscular Dystrophy Association on Thursday, and the weekends doing the usual things we did on weekends together.

On Friday 22 June, we went to a symposium on the Magill campus, on the topic Writings of War. Many of my closest work colleagues were involved in the symposium; some had met Ben a few times before, and some met him that night for the first time. That so many of them would be attending his funeral service thirteen days later was the last thing on any of our minds that evening, as I stuffed salami and camembert cheese down both our throats at the closing drinks. (About thirty of my colleagues, former colleagues and former students were among the more than two hundred people at his funeral.)

On the way home, Ben spoke freely about the seminar. Some of the talks he considered academic self-indulgence, and said so. But overall, he was stimulated and interested by what he had been listening to, and what things it had made him think about. As his obituary in the newspaper noted, he listened with particular interest to a talk about letters from wounded World War I servicemen, and how the nurses had to write these letters for those soldiers who had had their arms or hands blown off. We learned the sobering fact that 150,000 Australian soldiers were wounded during the Great War, and about 90,000 of them sustained lasting physical or mental disabilities.

(I probably saw some of those old diggers with my own eyes. In the 1950s, the bus from my grandad's home to the city would take us past an old sandstone building used as a repatriation hospital in Randwick, NSW. My grandfather pointed to the faces in the windows, and told me that some of these old soldiers had been there since Gallipoli, forty years earlier. Such spans of time were incomprehensible to my child's mind then, but the image of their faces in the windows has stuck.)

Soldiers needing nurses to write for them... Whatever the specific, clinching reason, the day after the symposium, he decided to buy a voice recognition program for his computer. The time had come when Ben knew he no longer had the strength to use a computer keyboard. I knew that he couldn't move his hands across a normal-sized keyboard, but it still shocked me to realise that he had to make an effort now to depress the individual keys, even if his hand was lying on them. A friend had observed Ben texting on his mobile phone a week or so earlier, and had commented to me that the only downward pressure Ben was now exercising on the keypad was the weight of gravity. Ben made no fuss about this with me. He said nothing about how he must have been feeling. He just took a decision, and decided to deal with it as best he could. Hence the trip to the computer software shop.

That Saturday night, Ben was in a talkative mood. We had always talked sport and politics, but he had become more and more interested in philosophy and religion. These talks about the meaning of life would often take place when he was in his bed in my room, and I was in mine a few metres away. He would do most of the talking; my contributions were more in the form of reaffirming grunts than coherent sentences. More often than not, I was too tired to think, yet happy and at peace listening to him as he talked to me. While there's words, he is there, with me. (As I write this, I realise there must have been many nights when he fell asleep while I was talking, and vice versa.)

Anyway, on that last weekend, it was 3 a.m. by the time he was done with talking, and we finally went to sleep. That Sunday, I was too groggy from lack of sleep to do anything much except get through the day doing as little as possible. I spent the afternoon dozing on the lounge room sofa while Ben watched the footie on TV. Prime Minister Howard had just announced his intervention into Aboriginal communities in the Northern Territory, and Ben was interested in the pros and cons of this drastic decision, and wanted to talk about that.

On one of those last weekends, we had also watched a *60 Minutes* show about disability and life choices: whether foetuses with these kinds of crippling diseases should be aborted in the womb; whether people in Ben's position should have the option of assisted euthanasia available to them. The person interviewed had some form of muscular dystrophy, such that every time he swallowed liquids, he was at risk of drowning. It was harrowing viewing, and I suggested we might change the channel, but Ben wanted to think these issues through. I don't recall him making a comment about euthanasia, but I do know his opinion on the former topic: He thought the arguments that he should have been aborted in the womb were as strong as the arguments against.

I come back to the final day. I had wanted him to arrive at my house via Access Cab a little later in the day; he had wanted to come a little earlier. He came a little earlier. I know from what he told his mother that he was pleased with this little bargaining success with me. Whatever, the Access Cab pulled up early in the afternoon of Tuesday 26 June. It was a brilliant winter's day; my north-facing backyard was warm and sunny. Crystal, the family dog, was at my place, and got herself up into her usual position when she saw Ben again – in his chair, on his lap. They spent about half an hour like that, parked in the sun, taking in a few rays, while I kept working away on a report I was writing for work.

Eventually, he wanted to come inside. After I set him up with his computer on his tray, he asked me to insert the voice recognition program CD ROM in the drive. I did so, and returned to my own work in another room.

I jumped up out of my seat at least a dozen times that afternoon. For nearly twenty years, responding to Ben's voice had become a conditioned reflex, a sign that he needed something that he could not do for himself, a call to immediate action for me or his mother. But that last afternoon, he and I lived out our own comic version of the old aphorism that history occurs first as tragedy and then as farce.

For the first time in all those years, he wasn't calling out to me or anyone; he was learning to use the voice recognition software, and the words and sounds he was making were for the machine's benefit, not mine. Most of the words he spoke that afternoon were to a machine, and were for training purposes only. Nevertheless, I reacted each time, before realising what was going on.

That is how his last afternoon on earth was spent – beginning to learn to use this voice program for his computer, because he had to, because he knew he could no longer rely on his hands. Just like Huck Finn, he had reached yet another crossroads, and he was lighting out for the territory, ahead of the rest, going forwards, not looking backwards, dealing with his predicament, and moving on, making the most of the cards he had been dealt.

*

Three months after Ben had died, the French writer Andre Gorz and his British-born wife of fifty-eight years, Dorine, committed suicide together in a French village where they had been living out their retirement. He was eighty-four; she was eighty-three, disabled and terminally ill. A year earlier, Gorz had written an extended love letter to his wife, published in English in 2008 under the title *Letter to D: a Love Story*.

Gorz has written a moving book, about love, and about writing about love, and about what it means to live through writing. On page 81, a phrase occurs which the publisher thought important enough to use on the back cover of the book:

You gave all of yourself to help me become myself. (Gorz, p. 81)

I am transfixed by these words. I have been working for weeks on the complex intersections between family and culture that somehow came together for me through my life with Ben, and I have been unable to crystallise my thoughts, or even calm the febrile state in which they are going round and round in my head. Now, I have stumbled across these words, and I am convinced they carry a coda, something that will help me untangle the meaning of Ben's life, and also the meaning of mine. I stare at these words, trying to decode every hidden inflection of meaning in them.

I can see a truth in the first clause: 'you gave all of yourself'. And I can see a truth in the second: somehow you did 'help me to become myself' – more than anyone else in my life has helped me. But how and what exactly, and how are the two clauses linked?

I dismiss any grand redemption narratives out of hand. Jesus Christ might have given his life so that we might live, but enough is enough. I don't want any messianic meaning-making giving me meretricious comfort. The idea that somehow my son might or did live the way he had to and then die, that I might live, is an outrage to everything I want or believe in. I also reject any implication that the meaning of his life can be found in helping me to work out what the meaning of my life is. Romantic nonsense, not to mention absurdly inappropriate for a relationship between a father and his son. Yet both parts of this couplet are true. Benjamin did give everything he had; and I do believe he helped me, more than any other human being, to become myself. But how? And what does it mean?

A quick Google of 'father and son' sends my thoughts flying in a million directions: the two George Bushes (the stuff of bad dreams), sundry crimes involving fathers and sons (fathers shooting sons, and vice versa; clearly, Oedipus lives on), the lyrics of the Cat Stevens song (highly irrelevant for me at that stage of life), and links to the Edmund Gosse novel that I had read and been bored by as an undergraduate in a Victorian literature class. I jump to *Dombey and Son*, but this is not right either, although I sense that I am getting closer.

Then I start to get it. D.B. Galvin and Sons. Donald Bede Galvin (1889–1977) was my grandfather, the reason why Ben's second name is Bede, and he was still in business with his three sons, including my father, for most of my childhood. The first three or four places I lived in were owned by D.B. Galvin and Company, not by my parents. And likewise the shops they earned their living in.

I come from a family of small business people – men and women who, once they moved from their Irish and then Australian family farms, were not middle-class enough to be professionals but not working-class enough to work for a wage for someone else. I come from a culture where fathers and sons were not restricted to a private, personal identity in relation to each other; they also had a social, public relationship. I come from a culture where fathers worked with sons, and sons worked for their fathers, as a matter of course. Even though that form of working relationship has been severely shaken in my generation, and now seems iconoclastic, not to mention nepotistic, in the context of places like universities and concepts like careers, it is still very much a social fact. I Google a common name, 'Brown and Sons' and get over sixty million hits. I try 'Woods and Sons' and get over eighteen million hits. I Google Galvin and Sons, and get 455,000 hits, the first two being a building firm in County Kerry and a builder in Jersey in the UK. I Google Michael Galvin and Sons, and get 45,300 hits, the first one also a builder in County Longford, in the middle of Ireland, halfway between Galway on the west coast and Dublin in the east.

Once Ben had left school, and his parents had separated, all sorts of possibilities became apparent that were hidden from view while those other two mountains seemed so solid. I came to realise that we got on in the kind of way a father and son might, if the son was to follow as an apprentice in his father's trade. It was not to be, of course, but I experienced enough to know how satisfying it might once have been, in other times and places.

So this is how Ben helped me to become myself. I learnt to acknowledge the price there was to pay, inside myself, for losing a big chunk of my ancestral, tribal identity and culture. It's a romantic daydream now of course, and not only because Ben is gone, but that does not stop me imagining a life working with my son, gradually watching his authority and competence wax as mine wanes, playing my part in passing the baton of life to the next generation, at ease with the world and my and his place in it. An ordinary working life spent chatting about matters great and small, sharing knowledge and experience, and finding humour and droll interest in the same kinds of things. And if there were grandchildren, one of the reasons I would enjoy them so much is because I would know from my own experience how much happiness they would be giving my son.

This is a fantasy about the present or the future, of course, but it is my prehistory, what has been encoded in my make-up for many generations. My own history, I know well enough. Somehow, having an adult son that I got on with like I got on with Ben has helped me to synthesise the two: the prehistory with the history.

There have been Michael Galvins in our Australian family tree since 1841, when Michael Galvin, twenty-six years of age, sailed, along with 221 other assisted emigrants, two hundred of whom were Catholics, from Plymouth into Sydney Harbour on the barque *Runnymede*, arriving on 30 August. Within three years, his fiancée had also arrived, they were married, had bought land at Yass, NSW, and had given birth to the first of their nine children. There are three generations between him and me, and the eldest son in each was called Michael. Now I am the only one left; it is not a tradition that has continued in my family.

I am wearing a gold ring, with the letters MG embossed on it. I had given this ring to Ben for his twenty-first birthday, and will pass it on in due course to the cousin Ben decided should be its bearer after him. The ring was given to my great grandfather by his eldest son, who had the ring made from a nugget of gold he had found on the West Australian goldfields in the early 1890s. That same eldest son also had a son, who died in Burma as a prisoner of war of the Japanese in 1943. His death caused the ring to shift to my grandfather's line of the family, and it was given to me by my uncle and godfather, on the occasion of my fiftieth birthday. He had been the keeper of the ring since his twenty-first birthday, in 1945.

The point of this digression into family trees and golden rings? It is simply this. For a few years, I got to know and enjoy Ben in a way that most fathers will never get to know their adult sons. And through this knowing, and forced intimacy, I recognised better who I was and where I came from – the parts of me that an 'education' and a 'career' and a 'cosmo-multicultural lifestyle' obscured from view; the parts of me that have more in common with my great-grandfather and his father than with my closest professional friends. The price for this knowledge? For this happy and satisfying relationship with my adult son? His disease, his disability. Yes, the sad truth is that his disabilities were the necessary if not sufficient condition for the intense relationship we had, and the unforeseen lessons this had for me. Able-bodied, Ben could and would have had mates and girlfriends his own age, and would not have needed his father, as we discussed on many occasions. My main role would have been as his grumpy old father, left to do my own thing, while looking on from the sidelines (hopefully admiringly) at his unfolding adult selfhood.

I am reminded of the words Ruth Cracknell used when the day of her husband, Eric's, funeral arrived:

This day is impossible to anchor in any identifiable reality. No template. (Cracknell, *Journey from Venice*, p. 7)

A son with Duchenne muscular dystrophy. Over a twenty- year period, I have lived through hundreds of difficult days for which I had no template, no identifiable reality to anchor my experience. Each was a one-off. And yet, here in his last few years, I had glimpsed an ancient template: father and son, son and father. The template may be an ancient and atavistic one, but I recognise it nonetheless, and the unexpected comfort and identity to be gained from it. I had the good fortune to have a relationship with my adult son that I had never anticipated while he was growing up, and which makes my daily life now, without his tone of voice and turn of phrase and bemused expressions, intolerably empty. Without the sound of his voice, my hearing will never be the same; without his big ears to hear me, I don't sound the same either. His voice is lost, but so is the most important one of mine.

9

Aristotle Makes a Statement

It is a beautiful early autumn afternoon in Sydney, and I find myself walking through Victoria Park, an inner-city oasis adjoining Sydney University, the university's own imposing sandstone Gothic buildings partly visible through the Moreton Bay figs that grow well in many of the old Sydney parks that have been intensively 'gardened' for a century or more.

Walking past the artificial lake in Victoria Park, whose evolution from a featureless concrete water 'fountain' to natural bushland sanctuary is something I have witnessed since my own days as a student, I comment on the abundance of bird life in and around the lake and on the bushland island. The place is teeming with the sights and sounds of swans, ducks, and ibises. The ducks in particular grab Christine's attention, and she again tells me the story of her schoolgirl experience in Western Springs, a similar park in Auckland. The main things I know about her childhood are her loneliness and isolation, the inner life of a girl who took comfort from a cruel world by befriending abandoned animals. A Malaysian Chinese father, a Japanese mother, and a new life begun in New Zealand as a teenager – one of the millions of ethnic, migratory hybrids that are part and parcel of the transnational ethnoscape at the end of the twentieth century.

I am in a mellow mood. I am thinking about the cute ducks, including the one she saved from danger in Western Springs. Images of the heartless stranger who took the duck away from her are filling my mind. 'Yes, I was so looking forward to taking it home and cooking it.'

I inwardly chuckle at my own sentimentality. The thought that she was befriending the duck for the purposes of eating it, not saving it, and was only prevented from doing so by a responsible citizen, not a creep, had not entered my mind.

Forty years ago, the only direct entrance from this park into the grounds of Sydney University was through a small gap in the cast-iron fence – the bars had been bent, to create a short cut to mark the major Broadway bus stop on the other side of the park. But now, in March 2008, I find that a far grander entrance has been erected now in stone, and a major gateway has been created, linking the patrician university grounds with the egalitarian public park next door. We walk up the steps, and are inside the silent grounds of one of Australia's best sandstone Gothic theme parks. The light is autumnal now.

Sydney University, take one: 1969. My most productive year as a student. Halfway through an Arts degree. Far enough into the curriculum that the place had become comforting and familiar; far enough from the end that it was still an all-encompassing world in itself. My twenty-first birthday halfway through the year, and I am looking now at the collection of T.S. Eliot's poems that one of my friends gave me then. The late-afternoon light of London that Eliot describes reminded me then of this time and place, and still reminds me now. I used to prefer late afternoon tutorials, when I could come out of the classroom at dusk, walk through the old quadrangle, and suddenly see the CBD of Sydney before me, alive and humming, as twilight changes into dark, and office buildings light up. Eliot's violet hour, when everything is ready, everything seems to be on the verge of something.

Sydney University, take two: January 1998. Had this grand gate-way from Victoria Park into the campus been built then? Even if it had, it would have been of no use to Benjamin and me, because there was a short flight of steps to negotiate, and no accessible ramp. Benjamin and I have spent a hot summer's day walking around this part of the city, before arriving in the vicinity of the university. Paradoxically, once he had become permanently confined to an electric wheelchair, doing things like this with him had become much easier and more relaxed. While he was still on his feet, there was the constant worry that he would fall, or be knocked over. While he was in a manual chair, there was the constant need to hold and push, to be on the alert for slopes or obstacles, to stay glued to his back, to give up any individual sense of personal space, for him or us. Esther and I had many talks while pushing Ben in a manual chair, but none of them could be about him, or about our hopes and fears about him, or about any other topic that it was inappropriate to discuss without Ben being a part of the conversation.

When it finally happened, being confined to an electric wheelchair was a liberation for Ben and a relief for me. He could go more or less at his own pace, and he could go more or less where he wanted to on his own, which he often did. I could walk more often at my own pace, and be in my own skin at least some of the time.

Sydney 1998

Our family trips to Sydney were usually packed with activities and outings, and this one was no exception. As Ben moved into his teens, our common interests merged, and we spent more and more time doing things that fathers and growing sons do.

We were there at the SCG to see the last day in Mark Taylor's test cricket career. All around us, the barmy army, the legions of English cricket fans urging their team on, kept up a constant assault on our hearing. Closer to us, I noticed an elderly man doing his best not to draw attention to himself, quietly assisting his wheelchair-bound son to urinate into a bottle at the back of a cement passageway in our grandstand. The bare concrete was awash in spilt beer and rubbish: the accessible toilet was too hard to get to from where they and we were perched.

There were many great days like this. When Ben and I would head off in the late morning from wherever we were staying, and not be back before nightfall. Our wandering excursions would last up to nine or ten or more hours. We would have a general plan, a kind of conceptual overview, but then improvise freely once we had started. Sydney, Melbourne, Auckland, Mildura. These are the places I most remember spending happy days like these, even if it did get to the point, in his last five years or so, when it was only possible to make such excursions in mild or warm weather. Cold, wet weather became a feared adversary. On the one hand, the risk of getting a sore throat or a runny nose was too great; on the other hand, his fingers would get too cold for him to be able to work the controls on his chair. Esther devised many ingenious ways of trying to keep his hands and fingers warm, but it had reached the point long before he died that he couldn't even take himself off on his own to the beach esplanade a few hundred metres from our house at Glenelg unless it was a warm, dry day. I never asked him how he felt about losing his much-loved trips to the beach in winter, when the storms were at their best.

My Sydney University experience proper began in 1968, and had finally spluttered out by 1985, the last year I taught a literature class in the Woolley Building on campus. Benjamin's Sydney University experience lasted less than one day – one hot January afternoon in 1998. From Central Railway, we had taken the light rail to Wentworth Park in Glebe, and set out from there. We covered much of Glebe and Forest Lodge, suburbs I knew well. The Catholic church in Forest Lodge – where my parents were married, where I was baptised, where my sisters were married, where Benjamin and Rosanna were baptised. This is a part of Sydney where nearly every street tells a story for me. I was fifteen when I first walked the length of Glebe Point Road, with a dim but growing awareness that life in these streets, many of which led to what was then a still active waterfront, was in a different universe from the newer Sydney suburbs most of my childhood had been spent in.

Some of this social history still clung to the area in 1998, when Benjamin and I explored the area, and I had a deep sense of satisfaction – at being able to talk to Benjamin about this mix of the personal and the social and the political, and knowing he was interested, knowing he was 'getting it'. It was an interesting day, but it was also a hard day. I was at first surprised but then increasingly angered by what a difficult suburb Glebe is to get around in if you are in a wheelchair. Cut kerbs were few and far between; the ones that did exist were perfunctory at best. Decades of Labor local government, I thought, and this is how the wheelchair-bound are still treated. Many times that day, we had to cross streets by using the closest car driveway to the corner, and heading onto the actual narrow roadway itself, dodging moving and parked cars. I was exhausted from the effort of nudging the wheels of his heavy electric wheelchair out of ruts and cracks, and over rims and edges.

We had a kind of plan for the day. Take the light rail to Glebe, and head towards Sydney University. There is a pedestrian overpass across Parramatta Road which links the suburb of Glebe with the central part of the main campus, and we headed in that direction, stopping frequently for drinks and rests because of the heat. (We both needed the drinks, and I needed the rests.) By the time we got to the overpass, I was not in a good mood to be confronted by an impossible obstacle: steps at both ends of the footbridge prevented anyone in a wheelchair from using it. We were stuck across a busy road from the campus, and had no choice but to go about a kilometre in either direction before we would get to an entrance to the university we could use. These things make me angry, even if it is an overdetermined anger, the expression of accumulated frustrations building up over time. But it is still wrong that someone in a wheelchair should be so routinely 'planned out' of public institutions. I was disheartened, and felt like giving up there and then. But we pushed on.

Half an hour later, the long detour negotiated, we were finally on campus, and doing our best to get around. Like Adelaide University, Sydney University is not wheelchair-friendly. I showed Ben places on campus that held memories for me. In the refectory in the Student Union building, I showed him the extraordinary *Mankind* mural which was being painted slowly by Vergil Lo Schiavo when I was a student. Did he fancy himself as a latter-day Michelangelo, I used to wonder, watching him at work while eating a meat pie between lectures. As the union's own promotional brochure describes the process I had been witness to,

> In August 1970, Lo Schiavo began his paintathon which was to result in the largest mural in the Southern Hemisphere. Perched high on scaffolding erected in the Refectory, he worked through the noise and vibration of a hundred lunch hours. About to finish an eye or paint a cross on the horizon, the 61 year old artist at times felt that maybe it wasn't worth it. There were critics. His painting was even called obscene in an edition of the Union Recorder. He therefore went on strike until the author of the article apologised after considering possible legal action against him.

After the mural, I showed him places like the Latin Room, and the History Room, and the other nooks and crannies in the imposing quadrangle, including the stairway to a converted broom cupboard which I briefly occupied in the bell tower while a graduate student. Faces of people came back to me – people I either knew well enough or knew of. Nicholas Enright, Martin Johnson, John Forbes. Dead now, young then. Poets and classicists – the kind of flamboyant, earnest young men I associate with the north-east corner of the quadrangle, in the rooms and walkways near the jacaranda tree.

We finally arrive at the Philosophy Room. I stroll in, don-like and cocky. Benjamin feels less at ease. He is an adventurous spirit, but his sense of propriety is offended. It makes me realise yet again just how forbidding and unfriendly these institutions are for outsiders. I don't remember the details of what we talked about, but I do remember what I did. I picked up a piece of chalk, and wrote on the blackboard, 'Anyone who gives a lecture in this room is a jerk.'

Benjamin was shocked and amused in equal measure. He was keen to get out of there as quickly as possible. The words were stupid, and written on impulse. I have no idea why I wrote them. Maybe there was an element of deep-seated resentment, a feeling I have sometimes had that my putative 'brilliant career' never quite happened because, at that particular point, I was adjudged not to have 'the right stuff'. What went on at Sydney University may have been my gold standard of academic career benchmarking once, but even by the time I was in my thirties, I was well and truly over it.

Whatever the motives, Benjamin and I beat a hasty retreat from the Philosophy Room, failing to notice the statues of the two Greek philosophers standing at the back, waiting for the next generation of curious students to find their way onto campus at the end of summer just as I did all those years ago.

That was in 1998, and Benjamin still had another five years in high school. Now, it is autumn 2008, and nearly a year since he died, and everything is different, and I am walking into the Philosophy Room again, and this time the statue of Aristotle stops me in my tracks, and any thoughts about the Chinese and their liking for roast duck, or lonely Asian childhoods spent hiding in Auckland parks, slip from my mind.

Aristotle. At the time of his death, Benjamin had a couple of books on loan from the Unley Mobile Library. A few days after he had died, we had to clean out his things from the room he slept in at the Julia Farr Centre. On a table next to his bed, I found a book – a library copy of the complete works of Aristotle. I held the heavy book in my hands, amazed that Ben would have requested this of all books, knowing that he could never have held it up to read it.

Of course, there is no simple connection between Benjamin at fourteen years of age watching his father write graffiti on a blackboard in the Philosophy Room at Sydney University, and the twenty-two-year-old young man who made the effort to borrow Aristotle in the last week of his life. None whatsoever. And yet. Dots are connecting. There is a clue here to Benjamin's emerging adult self, and the life he was growing into, a life that at least in part transcended the routine social exclusions that come with the territory of disability. He was making a statement, a statement that was the all the more significant in the context of the last weeks of his life.

There had been some grim moments during these final months.

Even though he was still in the SA team for the National Electric Wheelchair Sports (NEWS) competition, and played in the week-long competition in Sydney in April 2007, he knew this would almost certainly be his last time. Players with Duchenne's generally don't keep their place in the team as players once they have reached their twenties. Apart from the obvious reason (in April 2008, the teams paused to remember three players, including Ben, who had passed away since the previous event), older players with Duchenne's were no match for younger players with this disease, or players with other, less aggressive, forms of muscular dystrophy, such as Becker's. Ben knew this phase of his sports career was coming to an end. He therefore surprised me one day when he said, apropos of nothing in particular, that he intended trying out again for the team in 2008. Sensing my surprise, he added, 'Dad, somebody has got to keep the bastards honest.' He knew he was going down, but there was no way he was going down without a fight, or to make tough decisions any easier for the coaches.

My uncle Jack came to see Ben the last afternoon he played at NEWS in Sydney. Jack, my godfather and favourite uncle, living in a retirement home in Maroubra, had always had difficulty with his emotions when it came to Ben and his condition. That afternoon, my eighty-year-old uncle spent his last few minutes with Ben lightly and playfully shadow boxing him in the chest, man to man. We were saying our goodbyes. Jack dealt with his feelings by treating Ben in this exaggerated, macho way. It was a sign of unity in adversity, of the fighting spirit, of not giving in, of living to fight another day. Ben smiled broadly. Family, even distant great-uncles, mattered to Ben.

Knowing he was at the end of his time in the NEWS team was one of a number of low notes in Ben's last months. He was getting to the point where the limitations imposed by his physical condition were now so remorseless in their consequences that it was becoming harder and harder to work around them or compensate for them. Even modest dreams like some sense of independent adult identity looked less and less feasible.

For many years, Ben wanted to eventually live independently from his parents. He was sufficiently involved in the politics of disability to know that government was retreating from the negative consequences of large-scale institutionalisation on the one hand, and adopting the rhetoric of independent living in the community on the other. Whether enough resources will ever be devoted to doing this in a decent or holistic way is an issue I will not go into here. Big institutions, like the multi-storey Julia Farr Centre in Highgate, formerly known as the 'Home for the Incurables', and rebranded in early 2007 as 'Highgate Park', had gradually emptied as more and more people with disabilities were being relocated in various forms of small-scale assisted accommodation, sometimes after many decades of intensive institutionalisation, sometimes in distant suburbs they had no previous connection with.

Ben had friends living like this, and had been looking forward to a similar life at some point. But Ben also needed more physical care than most disabled people. He needed carers twenty-four hours a day, seven days a week. Such constant care is obviously expensive. But even if the carers could be found, and funds could be provided to hire them, there was still one big obstacle that gradually became insurmountable. We were driving in the van one day when Ben broached the subject:

'Dad, it's a bugger.'

This was the kind of conversation opener from Ben that had the potential to head off in any direction. He could be about to tell me that he didn't want to live anymore, or he might be about to tell me that a traffic lane was closed on the road ahead.

So, with some wariness, I replied after a few seconds, 'What's that, Ben?'

'The bi-pap machine. It's going to be the thing that stops me from living on my own.'

A bi-pap machine? I suppose this is one of those words which is second nature to thousands of people, as much a part of their daily vocabulary as dressing gown or mushrooms on toast, and yet an ugly and alien acronym, signifying nothing, for millions of others. It stands for 'bi-level positive airway pressure' ventilation machine, and is described on the manufacturer's website in soothing, non-threatening language, the language of promotional culture

> Effectively manages patients with breath synchronisation challenges associated with unique lung and chest-wall conditions.

To say that Ben had breath synchronisation challenges is one way of putting it, I guess. To say his lungs were now too weak to get enough oxygen in, or enough carbon dioxide out, and that this situation was now life-threatening, is more to the point.

For the previous five years, Ben had needed to use such a machine when he slept at night, or during the days when he was in hospital with a chest infection and needed extra assistance to get enough breath. The decision to begin using such a machine is taken by a doctor when the patient's lung capacity gets below a certain point. Ben's lung capacity was around 30% of normal when he started on the bi-pap, and below 20% (or less than half of one lung, as I would remind myself when he was sick, and he was exhausted and distressed from trying to cough), by the end. It is a steeling experience, taking your child to do a breathing test at a hospital, watching them blow into a tube as hard as they can, watching the percentage keep dropping (I think it was around 80% the first time he did such a test), and knowing how serious it all is.

For the record, from page 3 of the Post Mortem Report for Benjamin Bede Galvin:

RESPIRATORY SYSTEM
Nose, nasopharynx and nasal sinuses: normal in configuration.
Larynx: normal in configuration with intact, smooth and glistening mucosal surfaces.
Trachea and major bronchi: normal in configuration with mucosal surfaces covered by the usual amount of mucoid material.
Left and right pleural cavities: contained the usual amount of clear fluid. No adhesions found.
Left pleural cavity: contained ml [sic] of clear, pale yellow fluid.

Right pleural cavity: contained 25 ml of clear, pale-yellow fluid.

Lungs: (left 360 g, right 300 g), normal in configuration. Cut surfaces show congested lung parenchyma with oozing of the pink frothy fluid from the bronchial tree.

Pulmonary arteries: intact and normal in configuration. No pulmonary thromboembolism identified.

What a difference a word makes. How can I make sense of the irrational relief I felt when I read this section of Benjamin's post-mortem report and came across words like 'normal' (four times) and 'usual' (twice)? Benjamin died nearly twelve months ago. These words mean nothing. His heart, and then his lungs, collapsed, as totally as the Twin Towers did on 11 September. Yet even at that moment of total implosion, many of Ben's systems were normal, just as thousands of hearts and lungs were still beating and pumping normally, even in those seconds as the buildings fell down.

Is it abnormal to be obsessed with normalcy? I was an average child of the baby boomer generation, a primary school kid in the 1950s. For some reason, medical screenings, vaccinations and such like were taking place at school fairly regularly. (The icon of that period in Australian social history for me is the distinctive glass bottles that the government-provided milk came in every day at school. I can still smell their souring contents sitting in the sunny school playgrounds until late in the morning.) And it seems that in all those tests and screenings, I was average, normal, usual and so on. I was healthy in a completely unexceptional kind of way. I became so used to hearing the word 'normal' when I went to the doctor's that I am now quite taken aback if the doctor implies anything else.

And then, just as I am getting into my stride leading and living a good and normal life as the father of a beautiful, adorable, apparently healthy baby son, we learn one January morning that he is anything but normal, that he is about as abnormal as it is possible to get, that he has a disease that is making the paediatrician uncomfortable and even distressed as he glosses over what is in his mind as he tells us what this likely diagnosis means for our baby Benjamin.

Slowly but surely, Ben's results on really big things begin to deviate from the norm, they become the antithesis of normal, as far from average as imaginable, into a zone where normal has become a faraway land of receding memory and even fantasy: a spine bending to more than thirty degrees from average, lungs dropping to less than 20%, muscular strength in his limbs dropping to near zero. After years of coping with the stress and despondency of being told he was not normal, I craved occasions when Ben was 'normal'.

But everything is relative, including and maybe especially a word like normal. Abnormal things so quickly assume a new normalcy, it's scary. It is amazing how the normalisation of the abnormal becomes an iconoclastic form of familiarity and even a source of comfort. And so it was with the bi-pap machine in my life.

It seemed so noisy at first, and so fiddly in getting the face mask right, that I couldn't imagine how he or we would ever adapt to it, and the panic I felt initially took weeks to subside. Nevertheless, we all slowly got used to it and, by the end, I would find the rhythmic in and out sounds of air being pushed through it strangely comforting – a sign not of life being extinguished, but of my son's life carrying on. Its regular whooshing noise ended up giving me comfort during the middle of many long nights of interrupted sleep. I miss that noise now. I miss the feel of the mask in my hands as I attach the soft tubes to each of his nostrils and turn the noisy thing on.

But it is the bi-pap which Ben realises is going to be his biggest obstacle when it comes to his plans to live independently. Why? Because it is considered a technical apparatus, a piece of medical equipment, and the relatively unqualified carers who would be spending the night with him will not be permitted by their job description to take responsibility for such an important piece of potentially lethal equipment. Ben is angered by this technicality, and asks me why he is not able to assume that responsibility himself, thereby indemnifying anyone else from any consequences if anything goes wrong. I can only agree with him, but know in my heart that such a scenario is unlikely, and that the rest of his life will be spent either with me, or his mother, or in a large 'medicalised' institution like the Julia Farr Centre.

But I digress. The point is that Ben had good reason to feel moments of despondency in the early months of 2007. Whichever way he looked, he could see possible futures being blocked, for one daunting reason or another. But to say he was depressed is also wrong. He was still interested in living, as his last day made clear, and his vital signs were everywhere to be seen, for those of us who knew where to look and who took delight when we spotted them.

And one of the greatest gifts Ben ever gave me was the statement he was making with this book, found by his bed after he died. The complete, unabridged writings of Aristotle. Not just another Dan Brown novel. Why so?

When Ben finished his Year 12 at Unley High School in 2003, he did not see himself as university material. Because most of his active life was spent using a computer, hardly unique for a boy of his generation, it was predictable that he and we came to see his future as tied up in a technical kind of field (the irony in retrospect being just how ill-equipped he was for most of the technical aspects of information technology, but that is another story). And so it was that he completed a Certificate in Multimedia at TAFE in 2004, at the time hoping to get some kind of relevant, disability-friendly job on a keyboard when he graduated.

Nevertheless, another side of his personality and brain was slowly emerging during these years: the intellectual side. I think it began with the television news. It pains me now to think how much of Ben's life was spent watching television. But watch he did, often because it was the least demanding thing for him to do (for us, not him), and in particular the TV news programs. It was not uncommon for him to watch the 5 p.m. news, followed by the 6 p.m. news, then a current affairs show, and then the news again at 10.30 p.m. Thus he developed a keen knowledge and interest in politics and current affairs, both domestic and international. Politically, he became an angry young man, detesting conservative politics in general, and President George W. Bush and Prime Minister John Howard in particular. He despised their decision to go to war in Iraq. Michael Moore's kind of anti-capitalist, free-wheeling conspiracy theory thinking appealed to him greatly. Even in a room on his own, he would yell at the television set when some political figure he despised appeared on the screen. He was so incensed when Bush invaded Iraq in 2003 that he wanted to burn his American passport in public – a gesture I managed to convince him might not be a good idea for his mother or sister in the future.

By 2006, the upshot of this television education in current affairs was that he was seriously thinking about studying history and politics at university, preferably while his sister was still an Arts student herself. Rosanna was talking about him coming to some lectures with her in second semester 2007, so he could get a feel for what it was like on campus.

And so it was that, in late April 2007, he and I had enrolled in a WEA course in philosophy, and we turned up for our first class at the WEA building in Adelaide. On most evenings, the lecturer was late, and came rushing into the room with hastily photocopied notes tenuously held together under his arm in one big uncollated bundle. This was my first contact with the WEA in Adelaide. The classroom was full of a varied group of quiet, reserved people when we arrived, so much so that Ben and I were barely able to get inside the door. The room was seeped in introspection; there were none of the usual do-gooder smiles for someone in a wheelchair that you encounter in many public places, even if there were still the furtive stares.

I do not remember the lecturer's name. He had a big task ahead of him: to survey four thousand years of philosophical ideas, both from the East and the West, in six two-hour lectures. He was enthusiastic, and energised rather than intimidated by the magnitude of the task. I suppose it was inevitable that the lectures became a list of dates on the whiteboard, alongside of which someone's name, and then a single word or two scribbled alongside to describe their significance.

Heraclitus	5th CBE	change
Thomas Aquinas	1225–1274	scholasticism
Nietzsche	1900	nihilism

I struggled to retain my concentration, as my notebook full of doodlings makes all too clear, but Benjamin needed no such encouragement or props. He listened intently to every word that lecturer spoke. It took me a couple of weeks to work out what was going on. We had stumbled into a world where Ben was not just comfortable; he was increasingly exhilarated.

By this stage, Benjamin was spending his weekday nights and mornings at the Julia Farr Centre. On Tuesdays, he would come to my place by access taxi in the early afternoon, and we would drive into the city for the 6 p.m. lecture. After the class, we would have a meal before I would drive him back to his ward, where the staff would then begin the time-consuming process of getting him into bed. By now, the weather was getting cooler and wetter. It was a worry even finding somewhere to eat, because the distance between where I could park the van and where we wanted to eat had to be both short and under cover. There was a really nice pub we both liked the look of close to the WEA, but it did not have disabled access, so we never went there. Eventually, we decided on a small Indian restaurant in Pulteney Street, and we went there several times after the philosophy class.

No account of the highlights of Benjamin's life would be complete if I did not mention those few meals in the Indian Delights restaurant at the south end of Pulteney Street. Ben would be on a natural high. The lecture would have provoked so much curiosity in him that he would spend the whole time making obscure points, asking me impossible questions, drawing his own lateral conclusions. His mind was on fire. It was wonderful. I would be tired, worried, fearful, anxious to get him back safe and sound, and all Ben wanted to do, apart from enjoy the regular spoonfuls of butter chicken I would spoon into his mouth, was discuss the really big concepts and ideas. For instance, he passionately wanted to know about the history of belief systems in the Middle East, and believed that this was the key to understanding Iraq and the Muslim issues of the present day. Right or wrong on this point, his brain was engaged, fully and completely.

Even at the time, I was thrilled and satisfied. His academic interests were changing from history and politics to history and philosophy, and if he had lived I am sure he would have been attending lectures in philosophy at Adelaide University the following year.

In truth, he had lost much of what it was to be human in this society, or even a functioning animal, or even a machine in good working order. But he had not lost the capacity to think, to be curious, to want to learn, to think new thoughts, to suddenly realise (with feelings of relief, I think, as well as wonderment) that others long since dead may and do have much to teach us about the big questions in life, including our own life. Benjamin had found the poetry of education at last, as distinct from the dull and prosaic variety he had been exposed to for most of his school years, and I believe it gave him, just before the end, a new meaning, a new sense of possibility. I don't think it is going too far to suggest that Ben believed it might even be possible to make sense of his own condition if he could only find the right philosophical framework and ideas.

I am certain that the pursuit of knowledge would have occupied much of the rest of Ben's waking moments if he had lived longer, and I am also certain that it would have given him immense satisfaction and fulfilment. I am reminded of this on the day I am writing this down. I have had a headache all day, and the kind of dull dispiritedness that comes from a poor sleep. But I have the opportunity to attend a seminar, in which various celebrity bloggers are discussing the ways in which they think that blogging, and social networking generally, is changing the nexus between journalism and politics. Within five minutes of the first speaker opening his mouth, I am stimulated and engaged. My tiredness is forgotten. For all practical purposes, I have become a disembodied mind. I know Ben experienced this kind of intellectual exhilaration, this form of liberating disembodiment, in the last weeks of his life.

And so a kind of circle has been completed. From Sydney University in 1969 to the Adelaide WEA in 2007. My son and I had both found ourselves in the same kind of mental refuge at the same kind of age. When I saw the complete works of Aristotle in his room after he had died, I was able to make the link. Ben was making a statement about his life and about his future, and, without necessarily meaning to, he was making a statement about mine. More than a statement really, more a blessing or a vote of confidence from another world. All those years ago, I had chosen, more or less consciously albeit somewhat haphazardly, education and the pursuit of knowledge as my pathway in life. This last act of Ben's, when he borrowed this particular book from the Unley Mobile Library, communicated an important affirmation to me: that his father's choice had been a good one. He will never know how much that means to me.

10

Rip Van Winkle

Days pass, then weeks, then months. Some days, I can do nothing except go to my office, close the door and put my head on the desk. Tired beyond belief, but also a little astonished – surprised that the days seem to still pass, one by one, and I am still here, still nonsensically alive. His first birthday, in November, then the first Christmas, somehow come and go, and I'm still standing. A new year begins, and the need to diarise what I am living through, and what it all means, has taken root in my mind and is growing stronger by the day.

The final quarter

Walking down Glebe Point Road in inner Sydney in early 2008, my attention drifts to the extensive renovations taking place on the Valhalla cinema site. A picture theatre since the 1930s, an art house cinema in more recent times, it looks like its days as a celluloid palace are over. I read the developer's pamphlet:

> A sensitive development which will retain the existing shops, lobby and art house cinema atmosphere while providing fully functional work studios, each with timber floors and independent air-conditioning units. Some work units have terraces, courtyards, or mezzanines.

Buildings and their life cycle. Pictures for the working class, then films for students and hippies, and now ambient working spaces for the rising creative class. So it goes. But one minor scene is missing from this script – the few years in the 1970s when the theatre played host to a succession of over-the-top live musicals and performances, when Reg Livermore ruled over this glam world of extravagant costumes, language and ambiguous sexuality, when *The Rocky Horror Picture Show* first played here.

The Rocky Horror Picture Show

From my perspective, now, it makes more sense to speak of *Rocky Horror Shows*: first, Reg Livermore's memorable performances at the Valhalla in Glebe; then the movie with its cult following around the world; and finally, a 2008 revival, at the Star City Casino in Sydney.

I saw the original production in Glebe; I've watched the movie once or twice, including one balmy summer evening in the Adelaide Botanical Gardens in 2002; I saw the show again at Star City. Unsettled, I am having difficulty merging these three experiences into my personal narrative, how they relate to my life. Something is different, something has changed, something is out of kilter. If I didn't know it from looking in the mirror, I most certainly would by looking at the Valhalla being gutted across the road.

Three *Rocky*s, three moments in time. And the source of my confusion? Not Brad Majors, not Janet Weiss or a forever young Susan Sarandon, not Rocky or Frank N. Furter… No, the rising tightness in my chest and throat is focused on the mild-mannered Dr Everett Scott, Janet's high school teacher and sometime crazy scientist. And for one single, traumatic reason: Dr Scott is in a wheelchair.

When I first saw this show over thirty years ago, the sight of a wheelchair on the stage signified nothing. When I saw the film in Adelaide, the same image overwhelmed me. I was at that film with Benjamin, at a summer outdoor screening. We had to go to the back row so we would not impede the views of everyone else sitting on the grass. When Dr Scott came on in his wheelchair, I was not expecting it, and was shocked by the disconnect. By then, the emotions that a wheelchair now carried for me were intense and multifaceted. It was both lifesaver and dead weight. It gave my son the opportunity to get around, to go to movies like this, but it was also a sign of loss and worry. We had to deal with this heavy thing every day, whether it was getting Ben into a toilet, deciding where to sit, figuring out how to get anywhere. The needs of that heavy chair, and of the person sitting in it, were so all-encompassing that it felt like I was also attached to that chair by heavy chains. Ben's chair: pure heaven, pure hell.

It is hard to believe that I could ever forget a second time that Dr Scott was in a wheelchair. But I did. I am shocked all over again when Dr Scott comes wheeling onto the Star City stage. The wheelchair. A shock of recognition. A central star sign in my astrological universe for nearly twenty years, but now a black hole, a star that has ceased to exist. I see this wheelchair now and I feel empty, gutted, in a vacuum. I feel simple, unadulterated loss.

By 2008, I know that the myth of the wheelchair has colonised my subconscious, and any image of one, especially when I'm not expecting it, triggers a multiplicity of memories and contexts, and feelings painful and confused.

I last saw Ben's wheelchair a few days after he had died. It was in a dark storeroom not far from where he slept at the Julia Farr Centre. It looked empty and forlorn, like a dog that has lost its master and doesn't know what to do except wait. I touched and then smelled the well-used and somewhat oily headrest, the sheen coming from the thousands of hours that Ben's head and neck had rested there. Part of him still lingered in this chair. For some reason, it troubled me that the chair was left in a dark store room. It didn't seem right.

*

When I was turning fifty, I was happy to spin the tale of life being an opera in three acts, each of a quarter century or so. I didn't think I was fudging too much on the Biblical three score and ten, just adding a few more years to round out the numbers in a slightly more comforting way. At fifty, then, you have got to the end of the second act and are still in a position to look forward to one more full life cycle.

The overture to the third act of Puccini's *Madama Butterfly* is the perfect piece of music to sum up this feeling – that life may be two-thirds over, but the serious decline has not yet really begun (or can at least be plausibly unacknowledged), and there are plenty of vital signs that one might still be at or near the peak of one's powers. It is possible while listening to that overture to still kid oneself that you are forever young, and the world of make-believe, where dreams come true, is still enchanting. The tragic themes of the opera are momentarily 'caramelised' as they are reprised by the horns and other brass instruments. When I listen closely, I can feel all those childhood Saturday afternoons at the local picture show come flooding back again.

But about to turn sixty is quite a different matter. Even more grandiose and self-serving obfuscation is called for. Without fudging too much, you can convince yourself that your reasonable expectation, if not your right, is a span of eighty years. But life as a three-act opera doesn't stand up any more. More the case now to think in terms of quarters, and the advent of the fourth quarter is less comforting than the end of the second act. Even I know enough about Australian football to know that the final quarter is more often than not dull and boring. (As they say on the last Saturday in September every year, the third quarter is the grand final quarter.) The final quarter is often a let-down. When it is not, it is because a titanic struggle between victory and defeat is still going on. Who wants to live the final quarter of their life in such a state of tension, with the outcome still so much in doubt?

Some school friends had held a forty-year reunion a year or so earlier, and I had seen their pictures on the website. The only two that were remotely recognisable to me were the two I had stayed in touch with over all that time. Another sign of reaching sixty? For many if not most of us, the young man is hardly recognisable from the features of the old man. Somewhere in the previous decade or so, you have become detached from the people of your youth because, if they are alive, they no longer look recognisable as the same people living on in your memory from your shared younger days. And worse, you look at photos of yourself, and you can't see the connection between who you are now and who you were then either, with the then-you more the you you think you are now than the you you can now see looking back at you in more recent photographs or in the mirror.

I am nearly forty when Benjamin was diagnosed with Duchenne muscular dystrophy, and I am nearly sixty when he died. Twenty years. A generation. Things change. The Valhalla ceases its life as a picture palace, and morphs into a trendy office complex. For the first time in twenty years, I now have the time and energy to pay attention to all sorts of things that necessarily stayed below the radar for so long. I get a clue to my condition from photos of various parties that have taken place, of acquaintances from my earlier life in Sydney having sixtieth birthday parties and things like that. I look at them closely. All of a sudden, they look so old. And just as suddenly, I am hit by what I have decided to call my Rip Van Winkle hypothesis. They look so old to me because they, and so many other aspects of my life, were frozen in time for me twenty years earlier.

To be told by someone you have never met before, in a few sentences and without any prior warning, that your infant son sitting on your knee has a fatal disease that will kill him after forcing him (and you) to live for years with a destructive disability that will keep on getting worse right up until the moment of his last breath in late adolescence or early adulthood…such a sentence has no satisfactory capital letter to begin or punctuation mark to end. Life stopped. I stopped, although I didn't know it then. Everything froze, just like they say it does when you are in a car accident or a major disaster or some other life-threatening crisis. Many of my internal lifespan systems closed down, right then and there. The only meaningful reality became Benjamin's lifespan, and what was required to make the most of it, to survive it and, if possible, to prolong it. Any future beyond that future was repressed and eliminated, as all energy and focus was needed for what lay within this new time zone.

So, many of my own plausible life scenarios froze at that point in time and only seemed to turn back on again twenty years later, like this afternoon as I am strolling down Glebe Point Road and am trying to work out why I am feeling like I have emerged from some time warp. For twenty years, many of the things I could have hoped to do with my life under normal circumstances were obliterated from either possibility or consciousness.

And among the consequences: my friends had lived for twenty years and aged for twenty years and I hadn't even noticed it. No one, including myself, was allowed to get any older while Benji was alive. Kind of a reverse Dorian Gray kind of scenario. When I was nearly forty, I felt sixty, in the sense that many of the things I most wanted to do (like kick a football around in the backyard with my son) were now denied me. But when I was nearly sixty, I felt forty, in the sense that many of my expectations from life were still frozen at the time of Ben's fatal diagnosis. Neither age was natural or healthy. Both were caricatures of the other, as I was dimly coming to realise. A sixty-year-old with the expectations or appetites of a forty-year-old? Unnatural, and not really tenable. Somewhere along the line, long-delayed dreams become something else; parts remain intact, while other parts just rot away, or become malignant.

Welcome my son, welcome to the machine

Ben was a petrol head. He loved cars; his first word was car-car. Why he decided that he was a Holden man, I don't know. Maybe it was because we lived in Adelaide, and he had seen the factory where they build Holdens. Whatever, Ben belonged to that huge cross-section of Aussies whose idea of a great time is to go to V8 races and support Holdens against Fords, or vice versa.

The annual V8 race in Adelaide is known as the Clipsal 500, and Ben attended this event most years, with a carer (a family friend) who was as interested in car racing as he was.

As each month passes since we lost him, another event that he was interested in comes and goes. Each one is painful in its own particular way. The Clipsal race is back in town in February 2008, and I am invited to a party, in a house overlooking the track. I accept the invitation because the post-race concert is to be a performance by Santana, a band I have always loved.

The concert is living up to all expectations, even if I have been feeling the absence of Ben's presence at this place, for this purpose, all afternoon. Something is holding me back from fully enjoying myself. It is a warm, golden dusk. The sun sinks slowly behind the trees and city buildings, and Carlos Santana and his band become more and more absorbed and energised by their music. My sadness makes me hear all of this as if through several layers of insulating foam. Ben was at this event last year, and now he is gone. I have lost my closest mate; I am still living, still able to be at something he loved far more than me. It is a terrible feeling.

In the weeks leading up to this car race and concert, I had been reading Viktor Frankl, and here in the beautiful East Parklands of Adelaide, with Santana playing some of my favourite songs, their backdrop a panorama of gum trees gradually turning black as the sun's rays no longer reach them, Frankl's words about the redeeming power of love start to go around in my mind:

> I did not know whether my wife was alive…but at that moment it ceased to matter. There was no need for me to know; nothing could touch the strength of my love, my thoughts, and the image of my beloved. Had I known that my wife was dead, I think that I would still have given myself, undisturbed by that knowledge, to the contemplation of her image, and that my mental conversation with her would have been just as vivid and just as satisfying. (Frankl, pp. 38–39)

I had pored over these words when I first read them. Frankl tells us later that his wife and the rest of his family had already perished in the gas chambers, so I knew that when he came to write this, his wife was dead, even though he did not know it at the time when his love for her had sustained him in the camp. I also knew that Frankl was too sophisticated and realistic a thinker to be saying that this form of fulfilment through love could only come through romantic love between a man and a woman. I knew he was talking about love in general, love such as I felt for my son, love that was open to all people with the heart and willingness to love, not just lucky boyfriends and girlfriends.

Above the distant band on their stage in front of the river gums, above the large screens on each side of the stage, where Santana could be watched in close-up, above the violet city skyline, a plane flew slow and low from east to west, its lights on, approaching the airport. Higher in the sky, the stars were coming out. Among them, I noticed a bright light moving quickly; a satellite or the international space station, I assumed. Suddenly, Frankl's words and the Santana concert fused in my psyche. How?

To explain my leap of faith and hope that night, I have to backtrack. Even though Ben's interest in nature extended to the stars and galaxies in the night sky, and even though his childhood bedroom ceiling was covered in stars that glowed in the dark, I can't say that the heavens figured as one of his major interests or preoccupations. So, in the months since he died, it used to strike me as odd that I would find myself stepping out of my back door and looking up at the sky overhead, and fancy that I could see him glinting somewhere up there in the starry, starry night. A few moments looking at the stars would often calm my nerves and ease my grief.

Now, here at this concert, after feeling empty and gutted all day, I realise something. If it was just going to be Santana and me, it was never going to be enough. Neither Santana nor any other earthly experience was ever going to fill the gap that losing my son had left in my life. But what if I could use Frankl's words to reframe this experience, not just as a two-way interaction between me and some event in the present, but triangulated, as it were, with the mediating third party to this relationship being the love between me and my son, whether dead or alive? Could I trust Frankl's conviction, born of a sterner test than I was going through, enough to believe that?

What happened was this. Instead of focusing on a straight-line relationship between me and the stage, I imagined a human being satellite in the sky – my son, with all his history, interests and curiosity, all of my love for him, and all of his love for me, and his undying love for life in whatever form it took (he never, ever wanted to die) – a vast silver booster signal overhead. I imagined the sounds of Santana and his band going up into the sky, and then being reflected down again, bounced through my son, my own spirit in the sky, to me. And suddenly, I began to enjoy the music, to lose myself in its rhythms, to forget about my regrets for times passed. The emptiness I had been feeling all afternoon evaporated.

I had learnt something about the enduring power of love. For a few moments, I knew that Viktor Frankl was right:

> A thought transfixed me: for the first time in my life I saw the truth as it is set into song by so many poets, proclaimed as the ultimate wisdom by so many thinkers. The truth – that love is the ultimate and the highest goal to which man can aspire. Then I grasped the meaning of the greatest secret that human poetry and human thought and belief have to impart: The salvation of man is through love and in love. (Frankl, p.36)

Stephen Daedulus was a young man when Joyce granted him his epithanies. I wonder what staying power they have for an old man? Not much, I later realised. More often than not, the satellite connection dropped out. But it helped that at least it happened some of the time.

St Patrick's Day 2008

One year ago today, Ben and I had gone to an Irish pub in Marion, south of Adelaide. The place was packed. It was only mid-afternoon, and everyone already seemed drunk. I sat down on a bench, while Ben headed inside to check out the scene. A few minutes later, he came back out, his face scowling and angry. 'Dad, we're outta here. Some dickhead just patted me on the head and called me a retard.'

It reminded me of an incident in the Unley Public Library a few months earlier. We had also left in a hurry. A group of boys in their private school uniforms had stared at Ben in his wheelchair – to the point where he couldn't bear it any longer. Not embarrassment. Anger. Daily life for those in wheelchairs. If not pity, then dull, senseless curiosity. Ben was not one of those people who ever got used to being stared at.

A whole book could be written about staring. Or rather, being stared at. Few experiences are more threatening, as most cultures and even animal species know all too well.

Tuesday 18 March 2008

The menu at Stefano's restaurant in the cellars of the Grand Hotel in Mildura for the night begins with citrus and salt cured ocean trout, baby capers, beetroot and green salad, followed by steamed Boston Bay mussels, aromatics and grilled crostini, before moving on to Murrayland pork neck ravioli, sage butter and shaved grana, climaxing with Broken Hill organic lamb, baked polenta, carrots and baby cavolonero, and finishing with caramel pannacotta and local mango. Stefano has also selected the wines to accompany the meal: a 2001 Yarrabank Brut Cuvée, a 2006 Mountadam Riesling, a 2004 Lilydale Pinot Noir, and a 2007 Buller 'Beverford Gold' Botrytis Semillon to go with desert. We study the degustation menu with interest. There has been a cancellation. We can get a table if we want one. The price of $95 seems reasonable for the total package of food and wines. I am a little uncomfortable that the cellar restaurant does not appear to have wheelchair access. That cuts Ben out. But the whole thing seems just a little too excessive for our taste, and we settle for the bistro upstairs.

Two hours later, I have had a wonderful meal of flathead fillets (my grandad's favourite fish), and a couple of glasses of a crisp New Zealand sauvignon blanc, and I am feeling mellow and satisfied while walking back to where the car is parked.

I am in Mildura, and naturally, I have been thinking and talking a lot about Benjamin. The town is rich in memories, both my own memories of being with him on his own in 2004, but also from earlier times, when we were in Mildura as a family, either in transit to or from Sydney, or in Mildura for a holiday for its own sake. Mildura is a positive talisman for me. I feel his presence here, and also my presence with him, the person I was happy and lucky to be when I was with him. It is such a positive force that I look forward to getting to Mildura, of driving down the main road we have walked along, of seeing familiar motels, cafées and other landmarks. (I remember the excited SMS he sent to his sister when we went to see the wave pool at the local swimming centre on one of our trips together.)

I am walking back to the car, and turn a corner onto the main road, and am suddenly so sick in the stomach that I feel like I have just been kicked in the guts. Any lingering satisfaction associated with the flathead or the wine is dispelled in an instant. I feel devastated, the ground moving beneath my feet as if on a small boat in a rough sea.

I've just noticed something I had forgotten about and wasn't expecting. In the median strip near where we are parked, there is an ugly, squat public toilet block. It is difficult to get into if you are in a wheelchair, partly because it is in the middle of a busy road. On an earlier trip to this town (a trip I don't recall), getting Ben into and then using that toilet was difficult and stressful. Actually, I don't really know if it was all that difficult, but I do know that it was stressful, at least for me. Maybe the stress had more to do with my state of mind at the time, or the regular routines of broken sleep.

Whatever, I do know this: seeing that toilet block again when I wasn't expecting it brought back a dreadful, overpowering nausea.

That night is now memorable for me, not for the delicious meal, not for the Stefano gastronomic feast that almost was but wasn't, but for how sick in the stomach I felt. Sick because I have lost Ben; and sick because of the stress that was his and my life much of the time, like the stress of finding somewhere to urinate.

The great French novelist Marcel Proust writes somewhere that our sense of our previous selves, and our loves at the time, are more often triggered by trivial, not important, events. Proust is absolutely right. Yes, it is the trivial event, the involuntary memory, that can have the most impact and resurrect old selves and ghosts.

That night in Mildura taught me a lesson. Encounters with people, places and things that remind me of Benjamin fall into two distinct categories: those that are anticipated and those that are not. The ones I am planning and thinking about (like visiting his final resting place in Centennial Park) are sad in a positive way, and bearable; the ones that take me by surprise are mostly painful.

Ruth Cracknell has written about what I am trying to say here. Her unexpected time bomb was the blood oranges she fed to her stricken (terminally ill) husband while on a holiday in Venice:

> Fifteen months later I am watching an innocent cooking programme on television. The cook, Stefano Di Pietri, is bicycling through the Riverina, and he is going to visit a friend. It is the most idyllic of scenes, reminiscent of Tuscany. A meandering dirt road turns around a bend, revealing a splendid orchard of orange trees, and long before the cook cuts into the fruit I know they will be blood oranges and I am engulfed in such a deep and animal grief that had it been witnessed or heard, those not yet experienced in those matters would have been at pains to comprehend the spectacle. Minutes later, the tempest has vanished as erratically as it appeared. These are the ways of grief. (Cracknell, p. 120)

I had my first 'Cracknell moment' in Mildura nearly a year after Ben died, brought on by one of the ugliest public toilet blocks in Australia. I don't believe it is possible to describe what it is like until you have a sudden and unexpected attack of this deep, visceral grief. Why do I say this? Because I got through the first sixty years of my life before I experienced it for the first time, or could even comprehend it.

Once upon a time...

Benjamin and I spent six happy nights together on a trip to Mildura in September 2004. We had some great times. Eating sandwiches where the red Darling meets the grey Murray at Wentworth; exploring dry lakebeds in semi-desert to Mildura's south; trying the designer beers in town; watching football finals at the local workingmen's club. What it really meant for his parents to have separated hadn't really sunk in for either of us. If anything, I was still insulated by the sudden shock to my patterns and expectations of the previous twenty years. The depression that was waiting for me a few months later was still a small black cloud on a distant horizon. The thought occurred to both of us more or less at the same time: we actually enjoyed being away as two mates; we liked one another's company.

My last link with that bittersweet week was eaten a few weeks ago.

Although the motel was expensive (they often are if you need a room with disabled access), it was not very well equipped for our needs. The rails on the wall made it difficult to get his shower chair over the toilet. (We ended up using a bucket.) The bed was on low castors, meaning that I couldn't get the legs of the hoist properly under it. That first night, we decided to improvise. We walked along Deakin Avenue to the late-night shopping mall, and went into the supermarket, searching for something to raise the height of the bed so I could use the hoist and sling. We ended up buying six tins of beetroot, the idea being that the castors of the bed could sit on those tins, and be high enough off the floor to get the legs of the hoist under. It was a stupid idea. The tins were no match for the swinging weight of Benjamin in the hoist. I ended up positioning him onto a corner of the mattress, then slowly pulling him in his sling up the bed. And I ended up eating the tins of beetroot over a period of years, the last one this last summer.

7 April 2008

It is time. I am standing outside the auditorium where the South

Australian NEWS team are having their final practice. I sent an email about it the next day:

> Last night was one of the most difficult of my life. I got to the gymnasium in the middle of the team's final training session before the national series in Sydney next week. I stood outside, trying to muster the courage to go in. I could see the boys and young fellas in their chairs, the familiar whirring sound of electric wheelchairs in motion, the referee's whistle, the one or two people (like waiting taxi drivers) hanging about, the familiar faces. They were all there. Unlike Western Australia and Queensland, no more of our players have died since last year.
>
> In front of the parents (they were all fathers last night), I was unable to stop my eyes welling up with unbearable emotion and sadness. At first, I tried to pretend it wasn't happening, but then didn't bother after a while. I just sat there talking to them with tears in my eyes. A couple of them said how hard it must be to come back. Yes, it was. Fortunately, I managed to keep a brighter demeanour with the boys themselves, and chatted to the ones I knew a bit better than the others. This time last year, Benjamin was oldest and next cab off the rank. Now it is the next eldest, and everyone knows it, including him. Yet this idea of a death that is not very far off does not seem to make a huge impact. I wonder why. Ben used to say to me that he didn't feel anything when one of the gang died, and he used to feel bad because he didn't have any feelings.
>
> I wonder if the answer is because staying alive, able to move, eat, piss, crap and so on is so damn pressing and such an issue 24/7. The present is full of so many problems to solve that there is not much energy left over for melancholy.

In *Regeneration*, one of her great Great War novels, Pat Barker wrote about the officers unable to save their men from almost certain slaughter in the trenches of the Western Front:

> It was the look of people who are totally responsible for lives they have no power to save. (Barker, p. 107)

That is how the parents of these boys look. That is how I must have looked. I see in their faces what I was less than a year ago. They see in me what they will inevitably become in a future that is not very far away. I am becoming more interested in the First World War as I get older. The loss of young sons on a massive scale. So many parents feeling the loss that I am feeling now, and also for the rest of their lives. And the stress of this new kind of warfare on the soldiers themselves. And the words to describe their reactions to this stress: shellshock, nervous breakdown, war neurosis, neurasthenia. There are parallels with my situation. Barker describes the process thus:

> You're thinking of breakdown as a reaction to a single traumatic event, but it's not like that. It's more a matter of erosion. Weeks and months of stress in a situation where you can't get away from it. (Barker, p. 105)

Yes, exactly. I went through something like this. I finally cracked. It's one of the reasons why I find that trilogy of novels by Barker so difficult to read. I see myself in all those men who cracked under the pressure. My life wasn't on the line, my son's was. And his death was a certainty, not just a very high likelihood. And his worsening disablements were no figments of anyone's imagination.

I am pleased I have gone to support the team, but it brings less closure than I thought it would. They don't have the time or even the interest to think for very long about me. And why should they? I also know something I could share with them but can't: it's even worse than you think. Coping with muscular dystrophy seems very hard much of the time. But when your son is gone, it's worse, a million times worse.

But the world keeps turning, and two other things have been happening on this day, apart from my visit to the team for their final training session. One is front-page news around the world, while the other barely gets onto the news pages at all.

The torch relay for the 2008 Beijing Games has begun and is making headlines around the world, as large numbers of pro-Tibet demonstrators disrupt its progress through London and Paris. In Paris, an attempt is made to grab the torch from a disabled athlete, who becomes an instant hero in China because she will not give it up, breaking her leg in the process. And a small item on the ABC website states that the well-known Australian family therapist, Michael White, has collapsed while giving a talk in San Diego, and died.

How interested Ben would be in these events surrounding the Olympic torch. And how much I miss not having him here to discuss it with him. Ben was a proud Olympic torch bearer himself back in 2000. The fourteenth of July was a cold winter's day in the drab, hard suburbs on the featureless plains stretching north from the city in Adelaide. Ben carried the torch on this day, as part of the leg bringing it from the Barossa Valley into Adelaide. It was cold and cloudy, rain was threatening, his leg took him mainly past factories, where people appeared as if from nowhere to watch the torch pass. The excitement was palpable. I had been sick with worry about the logistics, but probably shouldn't have been. The whole thing went smoothly. An attachment was put on his chair, and the torch put into that. I could see that he did not have the strength to lift his flopping arm to reach the base of the torch, so I dashed out, and lifted his hand so he could grip the torch.

For once in his life, Ben was the centre of attention for 'normal' reasons. His face was transfigured with excitement and pride. People clapped and cheered as he went past. An impromptu crowd, including me, jogged alongside, cheering him on and clapping. All too soon, it was over. A young girl was waiting to take the torch from Ben, and the whole caravan moved on.

The months leading up to that torch relay had been hard. During the previous summer, Ben had had a major operation, to insert two steel rods into his back, running from the shoulders to the pelvis. The rods made him at least two centimetres taller, and also gave his body some stability, by preventing any further collapsing of the spine. The operation lasted four or five hours, during which Esther and I walked the hot streets of North Adelaide aimlessly, unable to enjoy anything or concentrate on anything. Convalescence was slow and painful. The torch relay had become something to look forward to, a circuit-breaker for the stress of these several months.

And it lived up to expectations. I knew something very important had happened. Benjamin had probably had one of the two or three greatest moments of his life. Something also snapped in me that afternoon, as I found out the next day on the flight from Adelaide to Kuala Lumpur, and recounted elsewhere in this narrative.

So Ben would have loved the politics and the drama of the Beijing torch relay eight years later. And he is now part of that particular eternal flame, stretching back and forward in history. He was the link in that chain for a few minutes as it passed into history, and that wonderful moment will always be his.

His life never got any better than it was that day. I proudly took the torch to work, where many colleagues wanted to have their pictures taken alongside it.

The loss of Michael White was also a footnote to the news in April 2008, and was also connected with another courageous moment in Ben's life.

By 2004, when my marriage had disintegrated, and Benjamin was struggling to deal with what this meant for him, on top of what it meant to be an eighteen-year-old male with his particular set of challenges, Michael White was arguably Adelaide's, if not Australia's, most famous therapist. He had become known around the world for an approach called narrative therapy, which I will summarise here, no doubt crudely, as an approach to family or individual crisis which stresses that, no matter how much one version of your own life story appears fixed, unchangeable and grim, there are alternative stories possible, not only in narrating what has been, but in imagining what could still be. It had become almost impossible to get in to see Michael by this stage of his career. Most of his time was now spent writing, researching, and running workshops in other countries. I think he agreed to see us mainly because of Benjamin's disability, and the issues this obviously brought to the surface for the person with the disability, and the rest of the family as well.

Benjamin and I saw Michael White at his Dulwich Centre premises for about half a dozen sessions in the second half of 2004. The main thing I can remember happening in those meetings was the way he was able to get Ben to speak about what it meant to be disabled. He could see that Ben's physical disabilities were having a major impact on his life, and that Ben was having difficulties accepting that he was really and seriously disabled, and what that entailed. (We had reached the end point of the long period of time when it could be pretended that his disability was not a huge issue, and that it could be glossed over while we went to great lengths to organise his life so that it appeared 'normal' for all practical purposes. That approach had worked well for many years, it had got Benjamin through high school, but it was now obvious that it had run its course. Ben's world was now the limited and resource-deficient world of the disabled, not because it had to be like this, not because he or we wanted it to be like this, but because the non-disabled world by and large is so unaccommodating of special needs of this magnitude. Try as he might, we were not living in the best of all possible worlds, not by a long shot.)

One day, Michael White made an offer to Ben. He mentioned that he was running a workshop in a couple of weeks' time, at which there would be about twenty professional counsellors from overseas as well as other parts of Australia. He asked Ben if he would be happy to come to the workshop and talk to the group on the theme of how his disability affected his life. This was a confronting subject, as Ben was only now really starting to think about and focus on this realisation himself.

Ben agreed, and I was there when he gave his talk. He spoke slowly and unemotionally about his condition, including what it is like to be in his shoes. The counsellors listened attentively and asked him questions. The session came to an end, and Ben and I made our way to a nearby pub, the pub we would usually go to after these sessions. Benjamin was exhilarated, on a real high – a high to match, perhaps even exceed, the ecstatic state he was in during the torch relay.

Three and a half years later, I am sitting in a city church in Adelaide, attending a memorial service for Michael White. There will be twenty or thirty such services in different places around the world, such was his influence and fame. I suddenly realise what Michael White had done for Benjamin. He had given him an opportunity to live his own courage through his disability, not in spite of it. By giving Ben this opportunity to speak in public, he had given him the opportunity to feel fear, to overcome fear, and then to feel brave and successful. This was more than just the terrors and then the highs of public speaking. This was acknowledging to yourself and to the world that you are what most of your life has been spent denying or ignoring: you are very seriously affected by physical disabilities you can do very little about, and these things affect everything about you. Ben grasped that opportunity, I am proud to say. Thank you, Ben. Thank you, Michael White.

Anzac Day 2008

We had talked about the dawn service, and we had talked about the march, but we had never gone to either of them. (Old habits die hard; my soldier father had never encouraged us as kids to take any part in Anzac Day ceremonies. Maybe one day I will, for both their sakes. My father and my son were undemonstrative quiet patriots, each cynical about how easy it is for politicians to manipulate nationalistic emotions for other purposes.)

However, we used to watch the big AFL game on TV. Essendon was Ben's favourite Melbourne team. I was more a sucker for the Last Post and national anthem, MCG-style, than Ben ever was. I watch it on my own this year, intending to visit Ben at Centennial Park once the match gets underway. I time my visits to maximise my chances of being alone with him. I weep when I stand there, and look at his picture on the plaque. I am not sure I would so easily cry if anyone else was there, and I don't want to have an experience of putting on any kind of front in front of him now, or ever again. I am soon to find out that Anzac Day is a busy day at cemeteries, especially those with large war grave sections, as Centennial Park has. We remember our dead, especially those whom age will not weary, including Ben.

I get out of my car. The military fields are near where Ben now is. And on every plaque a little Australian flag has been placed, and is blowing in the breeze. I count them. Fifty in a row, twenty rows to a section. And there are five sections just in this part of Centennial Park. five thousand shiny little Australian flags, fluttering in the breeze. I am stopped in my tracks, mesmerised by the sight.

I sit on the newly installed park bench near Ben, and begin to read a book. A young woman with blonde hair walks up the pathway, and stops next to Ben, bends down and puts a rose on his plaque. She recognises me the moment I recognise her. Cheryl, Rosanna's girlfriend. Here with her family to visit her grandfather, a returned soldier. We embrace, there is a tear in my eye, we say a few words, and she goes back to her family waiting by their car. I am reading Victor Frankl, and he has this to say about shedding a tear in the concentration camps:

> But there was no need to be ashamed of tears, for tears bore witness that a man had the greatest of courage, the courage to suffer. (Frankl, pp. 78–79)

Whether this claim is grandiose or not, I am not sure. But I do think this: crying may be many things. But to some extent, we can choose to cry, or not to cry, as the case may be. I now care less about crying, and more about not crying. I never ever want to not cry again, when the situation calls for tears. It has taken me a long time to reach this plateau, and now that I am on it, I don't want to fall off.

21 June

Ben was interested in all things meteorological – whether it was king tides, neap tides or dodge tides, summer and winter solstices, storm fronts or the playful scatter of light, fluffy clouds on a summer's afternoon. The year's shortest day has come around again. On this day a year ago, Ben had less than a week to go.

On this day last year, he took me into our backyard to make a point he had been thinking about. With the sun so low in the sky, what was the longest shadow my north-facing backyard fence was going to throw across my planned vegetable garden?

'Dad, look at where the sunlight stops. This is where the sun gets to on the shortest day.'

I measured it this morning. The shade extended eighty-seven centimetres onto the concrete patio, beyond the edge of the wet grass.

In recent years, my spirits had lifted a little bit each time the shortest day of the year came round. We were back on track, towards warmer, sunnier weather. It was a way off, but the days were getting longer again. And Ben liked and needed the warmer weather. This time I feel nothing.

26 June 2008

When I got to Centennial Park at about 10 p.m., I was surprised at how many candles were burning in different places, along with tiny lanterns flickering. I went and shone my torch at one. The woman had been dead for more than thirty years, yet still there was a burning candle that some-one had placed there and lit earlier that evening. A strange paradox presented itself. With all these flickering lanterns and candles, the cemetery felt much less dead at night than in broad daylight. The tiny lights create the effect of life all around you, not death. It is as if the dead are still there, just asleep, a great army of people resting there, still connected with the world of the living. For a moment, I felt as if I was walking among a medieval army, at camp, dozing or murmuring quietly, on the night before a stupendous battle. Agincourt, perhaps?

> Vigil, n. Keeping awake during the time usually given to sleep, watchfulness… (*OED*)
>
> Votive, a. Offered, consecrated, in fulfilment of a vow… (*OED*)

Shrine, n. Casket, esp. one holding sacred relics; altar or chapel of special associations; place hallowed by some memory. (*OED*)

When asked my opinion about what we should do to mark the first anniversary of Benjamin's death, I had suggested that we spend the time with him at his final resting place in Centennial Park, from when he collapsed at 10 p.m. to when he was officially declared dead at 12.05 a.m. We each brought candles; mine were half a dozen votive candles I had pocketed from St Francis Xavier's Cathedral a few weeks before for this purpose. And so for over two hours we kept vigil with Ben, burning candles all around his plaque and listening to music with special memories on my little sound system (mainly 'The Chariot' by Cat Empire and Pink Floyd's 'Wish You Were Here'). Rosanna and her boyfriend Tim didn't move from sitting on a rug in front of Ben.

We were all in tears some of the time; grieving, however, like three separate, solitary individuals, alone with our grief. We had become three stony Apostles, fragments of rock that had broken off from the mainland that the four of us had been part of once, our continent, now each facing the forces of the Southern Ocean alone. Towards the end, Rosanna did what she did a year ago at the final viewing of Ben's body in the chapel at Mitcham. She had the clarity of mind and strength of purpose to do what neither of her parents could initiate. She insisted we stand together for a few minutes, arms around each other, standing for what we were, Ben's family. She then said, 'His family meant everything to Ben.'

Yes, for Ben, family was always a whole that was far greater than any of its parts, and a whole that could never ever be broken up. Yet so much of the behaviour in our family life had been improvised, trying to decide what to do in the context of very different social and cultural backgrounds. I am reminded of how Barack Obama felt something of the same dilemma for himself and his siblings, that they were making up the reality of their relationships as they went along, uncertain of what bigger patterns of meaning they might exist in or use to make sense of their lives.

In this instance, I had thought we were still making it up as we went along, including what we did that night. But death had unlocked a deeper code. My often repressed Catholic heritage had surreptitiously supplied the script for that night's proceedings. The votive candles and the vigil. It hadn't been my own idea at all. As we walked out of the cemetery after midnight, it had felt right.

27 June 2008

And Port had said: 'Death is always on the way, but the fact that you don't know when it will arrive seems to take away from the finiteness of life. It's that terrible precision that we hate so much. But because we don't know, we get to think of life as an inexhaustible well. Yet everything happens only a certain number of times, and a very small number, really. How many more times will you remember a certain afternoon of your childhood, some afternoon that's so deeply a part of your being that you can't even conceive of your life without it? Perhaps four or five times more. Perhaps not even. How many more times will you watch the full moon rise? Perhaps twenty. And yet it all seems so limitless.' (Bowles, p. 212)

I am walking through the streets of Adelaide as the minutes tick down towards midnight. In a few minutes, 28 June 2008 will have arrived, and the first anniversary of my son Benjamin's death will have passed, not once, but forever. The fact that he has lived, lived and loved, will be forever a fact, I reflect glumly, as I stop in front of the Casino, remembering the Friday nights I have been there with him. Yes, those nights seemed limitless once, but there were probably only a dozen of them all together, not many, but enough for us to now talk about as an essential part of his life story.

I have had my own Paul Bowles moment tonight too, I reflect. I have just come from a performance of Mahler's Third Symphony by the Adelaide Symphony Orchestra. I have only heard this symphony in a live performance twice, I am sixty years old in a few weeks; this is in almost certainly the last time I will ever hear it live. It is a magnificent performance. The midnight song is sung by Ms Ning Liang, a mezzo-soprano whom the program lists as the Head of the Classical Vocal Department at the China Conservatory of Music. She is of indeterminate age, wearing a close fitting silvery/turquoise evening gown that tapers outwards slightly from the knees down, covering her feet, making her look a little bit like a voluptuous mermaid. She sings the song with intense and unwavering seriousness of purpose.

The emotional intensity in the hall is unmistakable. The terrible gauntlet that Nietzsche puts into words that are barely coherent and Mahler puts into heart-stopping music hangs in the air, like Damocles' sword, confronting and enveloping us all: that intense joy and intense sadness are intertwined, that you can't have one without the other, and that we wouldn't want it any other way. The juxtaposition of the smiles on Ben's face and the tears of those he loved bears sufficient witness to this truth for me.

My son's smiles have been extinct for a year today. That I have gone on living, that I can enjoy this music, seems an appalling travesty, a cosmic joke, a category mistake of the most elementary kind. One of the few consolations of turning sixty in a few weeks is that a smaller proportion of my own total life span will be spent bearing this loss. Parents who have lost a child – they know what I am feeling. There is nothing worse. The hell of losing one's son or daughter to war, disease, an accident or a suicide.

Another long journey is coming to an end. My journey with Ben during his life, and my journey with and without him in the year since he died. It seems somehow appropriate that I get a chance to listen to Mahler's Third Symphony again on this first anniversary. Twenty-two years ago, this very same music helped me cope when I first found out he had this crippling and fatal disease. I remember playing the midnight song, over and over. I remember one early occasion, sitting on my lounge, Benji, fourteen months old, standing unsteadily in front of me, holding my knee for support. A friend was visiting. We listened to this song in tearful silence. There was nothing to say. Twenty years later, that same friend's mind is so addled with early signs of dementia that she has forgotten whether Ben is dead or alive. A year ago, a few days before the funeral, she rang me to find out where the party for Ben was, and if he was looking forward to it.

It is now midnight. The clock is striking. Nietzsche's concept of eternal recurrence has been reflected in my own life experience, through this song, in a way that I could never, ever have imagined in a million years or a hundred lifetimes. I take the Penguin classic off the shelf, and copy out the version from my own ageing, yellowing copy of *Thus Spoke Zarathustra*:

> One!
>   O Man Attend!
> Two!
>   'What does deep midnight's voice contend?'
> Three!
>   'I slept my sleep,'
> Four!
>   'And now awake at dreaming's end:'
> Five!
>   'The world is deep,'
> Six!
>   'Deeper than day can comprehend.'
> Seven!
>   'Deep is its woe,'
> Eight!
>   'Joy – deeper than heart's agony:'
> Nine!
>   'Woe says: Fade Go!'
> Ten!
>   'But all joy wants eternity,'
> Eleven!
>   '– wants deep, deep, deep eternity!'
> Twelve!
>   (Nietzsche, pp. 243–244)

*

Scheherazade

This tale, my project for the last few months, is coming to an end. I feel a little like I imagine Mahler must have felt at the point in his Third Symphony when it is about ten minutes before the end of the final movement. Ending is hard, but the end is harder. Ending is a state, organically linked to the beginning and the middle; the end is an event, a final event, the harbinger of a new status quo yet to be born, or if born, grow. I think Mahler loved the experience of ending more than he wanted any actual end to occur in real time. Half a dozen times, the percussionists clash their cymbals at a climactic moment that seems like the end. But no, there is yet another final recapitulation and climactic moment still to come. How could it be any other way? 'A Symphony must be like the world – it must contain everything,' he had told Sibelius, his fellow composer. The end of any world is not a frivolous concept.

Writing this account has been driven as much by need as desire. The desperation of a man, getting close to retirement himself, struggling to survive emotionally, his nerves as worn out as old shock absorbers, wanting to make sense of the biggest things in his life – a life which included the rise, decline and fall of a marriage, a life lived with a son in the full knowledge that he had a progressive and terminal disability, and the sudden loss of that child at twenty-two years of age, a death that was as unexpected if time is measured in months or even years as it was expected and certain if time is measured in decades. My superstitions outnumber my honourable motives. I somehow cling to the crazy idea that, if I can keep Ben alive in words, I might keep him alive, or at least not dead, in other ways.

I am reminded of Michael White's brother and sister speaking at the funeral service for their famous sibling. While they spoke, the two of them often glanced at each other. For those few magical moments while they were talking about him, all three of them were still kids together, still playing in their Adelaide backyard, all still alive, and still to live. Perhaps this is why it was that I spoke for too long at Ben's funeral. While I was talking, he was still in the present tense for me.

Another wheel turns, another story I first heard a long time ago, but don't really 'get' until now. Scheherazade's story. As long as she could keep spinning tales to the sultan, she could keep herself alive. It worked for a while. Ben was still there for me in some way while I was writing this. So many stories I first knew with my head, not with my heart. Perhaps this is their point: to give us templates for the searing experiences that are to follow later in life?

These final sentences bring me no closure; no grand thematic recapitulations are suggesting themselves. I am still in the forlorn desert Isabel Allende found herself in without her daughter:

My soul is choking in sand. Sadness is a sterile desert. (Allende, p.9)

The sand makes me think of a beach, the beach at Glenelg. I am on the sand, and Benji is in the water. He is a young lad on his boogie board. He's going where the setting sun keeps shining, through the pouring rain. He's dancing beneath the diamond sky with one hand waving free. My boy. My boy in the prime of his short life. I can see him clearly. He's beaming, and he's free.

References

Adorno, Theodor, *Minima Moralia: Reflections on a Damaged Life*, London: Verso, 2005.

Allende, Isabel, *Paula*, Sydney: HarperCollins, 1994.

Arriaga, Guillermo, *21 Grams* (screenplay), 2003.

Barker, Pat, *Regeneration*, Penguin Books, 2009.

Barthes, Roland, *A Barthes Reader*, New York: Farrar, Straus & Giroux, 1983.

Bauman, Zygmund, *Liquid Modernity*, Cambridge: Polity Press, 2000.

Bergman, Ingmar, *The Seventh Seal* (screenplay), 1957.

Bowles, Paul, *The Sheltering Sky*, Penguin Books, 1949.

Benjamin, Walter, *Selected Writings, Vol. 1*, Cambridge, MA.: Harvard University Press, 2004.

Cracknell, Ruth, *Journey from Venice*, New York: Viking Books, 2000.

Didion, Joan, *The Year of Magical Thinking*, New York: Alfred A. Knopfg, 2005.

Dostoyevsky, *The Brothers Karamazov*, London: Penguin, 1972.

Eliot, T.S., *Collected Poems*, London: Faber and Faber, 1968.

Forster, E.M., *A Room with a View*, Penguin Books, 1974.

Frankl, Viktor, *From Death Camp to Existentialism*, Boston: Beacon Press, 1971.

Gorz, Andre, *Letter to D: A Love Story*, Pymble, NSW: Fourth Estate, 2008.

Kid, Thomas, *The Spanish Tragedy*, Oxford: Oxford University Press, 1998.

McCarthy, Cormac, *All the Pretty Horses*, New York: Alfred A. Knopf, 1992.

Milton, John, *The Complete Poems*, Penguin Classics, 1998.
Murray, Les, *Selected Poems*, Melbourne: Black Inc., 2007.
Nietzsche, Friedrich, *Thus Spake Zarathustra*, Penguin Classics, 1970.
Obama, Barack, *Dreams from my Father*, Melbourne: Text Publishing, 2004.
Rose, Peter, *Rose Boys*, Melbourne: Text Classics, 2001.

www.ingramcontent.com/pod-product-compliance
Lightning Source LLC
Chambersburg PA
CBHW030909080526
44589CB00010B/216